REFLECTIONS ON THE LAKES

By the same author
The Shining Levels

REFLECTIONS ON THE LAKES

John Wyatt

W. H. ALLEN · LONDON
A Howard & Wyndham Company
1980

Typeset by Yale Press Limited, London SE25
Printed and bound in Great Britain by
W & J Mackay Ltd, Chatham, Kent
for the Publishers, W. H. Allen & Co. Ltd.,
44 Hill Street, London W1X 8LB

ISBN 0 491 02601 3

Contents

Author's Note

I find it needs courage to open up old diaries. There is of course the pleasure of finding the amusing, the exciting, the successes, the human encounters; but these are plums in a stodgy pudding of frustration, the dross of routine, failure, work uncompleted. How does one pull out incidents from nineteen years of diaries and reports to provide material for a book? If I pick out the successes it would be an egotistical exercise (and the volume would be too slim). The amusing incidents only? Being a national park warden is often a very serious business. The drama? Too little of that. So I resort to a lucky dip. A 'Little Jack Horner' exercise.

Having chosen the interesting it might suggest that a warden's life is somewhat idyllic. This will raise wry smiles to the faces of my colleagues in other national parks and country parks who have reason to know that their jobs are no easy five days a week sinecures. I have not touched upon the wardens' routine chores: the rounds of committee meetings, the taking part in the painful process of decision-making in reconciling the need to preserve and the need to provide; the being a middle-man in disputes (and taking stick from both sides); the listening to complaints;

the patching-up and making-do with very limited resources, and putting up with criticism that the service is inadequate; and the odd working hours which are the ruination of family life. No matter. Many endure some of this or more, professionally or voluntarily, for the great satisfaction of serving the cause of conservation of our diminishing countryside.

I hope too that this book is about a national park, and not only about the doings of one of its servants. Reading old diaries can rekindle a warmth of feeling; and I have never reached the stage when I could not enthuse about forests, lakes or mountains, even when frozen or soaked to the skin. I hope though that I am not a sentimentalist. The countryside is so obviously beautiful to all when the sun is shining. Sometimes it rains.

To avoid embarrassment I have altered some personal names; and to avoid possible distress, in the accounts of mountain rescues, I have also altered locations and details.

John Wyatt, Graythwaite 1979

Prelude

One of my early memories is of the largest apple pie in the world. When I was around ten years old I had to travel to a Manchester hospital at regular intervals, and we used to go into the city by train. Waiting in the hospital was hell, but that journey there and back was a great adventure.

The largest apple pie in the world was across the line on another platform. I used to wonder what the huge apple pie was doing there, sitting upright in a large glass case in all its mouth-watering magnificence. It was definitely cram-full of fruit for its great crust was bulging, and every bulge was nicely browned. It was certainly sweet too because great pools of syrup filled the hollows. To a lad who was usually very hungry the sight was a sort of exquisite torture.

One day we arrived at the station for the return journey with time in hand, and trembling with excitement I went off to explore the distant platform and get a close look at that apple pie. At first I could not find it. When I did I was horribly disappointed. It was not an apple pie at all, but a large plaster-of-paris relief map of the English Lake District.

I had never heard of the Lake District. Where was this

land of pie-crust mountains and syrupy lakes? We certainly never learned about it in our geography lessons at school which seemed to be all about Africa and South America. In those days rail travellers could learn a certain amount of Britain's geography from the pictures in the railway carriages, because every compartment had several photographs of holiday resorts. I remember trying to get my tongue round Bettws-y-Coed, one favourite, though our particular railway line seemed to have an obsession with Pitlochry. But occasionally there was a picture of Windermere in the Lake District with the railway company's steamer packed with people. How could a lake be large enough to dwarf such a huge steamer? The only lakes I had seen were the old mill reservoirs. One, now included in a pleasure park not far from home, had a small steamer; but here was a boat that could take hundreds of passengers!

At this time I was a member of the 3rd Ashton Scout troop. Our rivals, the 1st Ashton troop, one memorable year had opted to camp in North Wales during the school holidays. Not wishing to be outdone, the 3rd chose to venture even more into the wilderness and go north to the Lake District. (There was no 2nd Ashton. Perhaps it had once gone off in some other direction and vanished into oblivion like the Roman ninth legion, never to be heard of again.) So we took our tents, our baggage, and a long train journey to Windermere where we were met by a big open lorry driven by a large man with a red face. Everyone seemed to have red or brown faces in Windermere and there was a clean tang in the air. We piled into the lorry and we were soon travelling alongside the tree-lined lake which we saw in great snatches through the gaps. Then up a hill and along a lane to a huge wood. There was a strange exciting smell; odd how easily one remembers smells – the smell of wet leaves and spruce resin, and the indefinable mixture of smells of lichen and cut wood; sphagnum moss and fungi; rich raw earth and meadow-sweet; elder blossom and cow-parsley. The smell of the forest, always changing, sometimes subtle, sometimes overpowering, but unforgettable. And it was all new and strange and very exciting. Somehow I felt as if I belonged. It was overwhelming. It was almost as if I had returned home after a long absence.

By nature I am a countryman. I have always been a countryman even though I was born in an industrial town. Every free moment was spent exploring what passed for countryside in our area. I remember too well the stuffy classrooms with the frustrating glimpse through the windows of the poplar trees in the neglected vicarage garden which was my first piece of wilderness.

All that seems aeons ago. But now here I am rummaging around in the rocks near the highest point in England. The air is clear and warm, and all around are the great reaches of soaring crags that speak of other time scales. We experience the 'passage of time' as if our journey along it has cosmic significance whereas it is only an infinitesimal flicker. It seems to have as little meaning as a dream yet like a dream it has its moments of excitement and joy. But from this airy perch, looking out over the far hazy humps of high hills, or westwards out to the wrinkled sea, there seems to be a vague hint of an explanation if only it could be read. It is perhaps a hint of belonging to something greater than the imagination can grasp. There is here an absolute and utter stillness, and not even a whisper of wind. Great immovable heaps of ancient volcanic lava and ashes. Frozen time, past welded into the present. In this place time is meaningless in human terms – a convenient invention. An imaginary line of hooks, perhaps, on which to hang one's memories and one's hopes. No, not a line, but a random collection of hooks, for it is sometimes easier to stumble on a memory of great age than to pick one up from yesterday.

But I do remember the first time I was sitting here on Scafell Pike and staring across a dizzy gap to the huge massive bulk of Great Gable, with mountains bunching away in every direction. No, I realised, not the colour of pie crust after all, but green and brown and blue and red, split by jagged ravines, with great rough ridges sawing into a clear sky, ribboned with spilling waters, brushed with a hint of drifting cloud. And I was here, having reached the perch, high above it all with my knees still trembling with exertion and excitement, with no thought of how I was going to climb down again. I kept a diary then, long since lost, but I remember well writing my first impression of Great Gable. It looked, I thought, with its huge hump, its runnels of red screes, its wisp of cloud, like a gigantic steamed pudding, just turned out of the basin, still steaming hot, the melting raspberry jam running down the sides.

I suppose such a description was adequate for a boy who found the sight of good food in plenty almost a spiritual experience. Wordsworth did no better. In his *Guide to the Lakes* he uses his sister Dorothy's words to describe the view from this same spot. 'We now beheld the whole mass of Great Gavel (sic) from its base – the den of Wastdale at our feet – a gulf immeasurable.' The poet is attracted by the gulf, the hungry boy stares up at the mountain. One down into the fearsome pit, the other to the free heights. Wordsworth explained that:

'Heaven lies about us in our infancy!
Shades of the prison-house begin to close
    Upon the growing boy'

I seem to have spent a great part of my life avoiding the prison-house.

Normally this peak is swept by great winds from the Irish

Sea, and scoured as clean as the Friday doorsteps of the town where I was born. But today it shimmers in the heat. I have at last finished rummaging and have pulled away a large pile of detritus watched only by my dog, whose panting is the one sound to break the silence. I have excavated a hole. The bottom of the hole is filled deep with sharp fragments of hard stone which is almost metallic. And there I find two-thirds of a Neolithic stone axe. Four thousand years or so ago the axe maker, having carefully shaped it here in this airy workshop, accidentally broke it and rejected it with disgust. It has lain on this spot, the chipping-floor, ever since. I do not know what sort of Neolithic noise he made to express his frustration. But I hold his sad message in my hand – a petrified oath.

Yet the axe factories were certainly a success. The view from here would have been different in his day. The tree line reached almost to the chipping floor. Gable would have bristled with tree and scrub, looking from this distance perhaps like a brooding giant in a bearskin cloak. It was he, the axe maker, who started the great change. His axe was no hastily made, primitive tool. Its shape was roughed out here, then carried down to the sandstone on the seashore miles away, where it was ground, sharpened and polished into a thing of precision and beauty. Fixed to its ash-wood shaft, the axe could clear the forest, push back the trees, shape the wood to build houses and boats. It was the first industrial revolution. The axe making was a large operation. The chipping floor I am sitting on extends for about four acres and is covered deeply with chippings. And this is only one floor. There are other known factories, and some yet undiscovered on these fells, all exploiting the vein of rock – a hard volcanic tuff – that threads its way through the high places from one end of the central mountains to the other. The Lake District stone axes were transported to many parts of the British Isles, and even to the European mainland. They have been found in large numbers in the south of England in the great centres of Britain's dawning civilisation. Pollen analysis of the deep sediment drawn from the lake beds gives evidence of the first marked decrease in the number of trees coinciding with the peak of production from the stone axe factories. The efficiency of the tool should not be underestimated. In the 1950s three men using true Neolithic axes cleared 600 square yards of Danish birch forest in four hours.

So the Neolithic axemen made the first changes to the face of the Lake District and the process has continued for four thousand years. With our new power saws and tractors we could clear all the forest that is left and all that has been replanted within a matter of months. We do not because we now treat woodland as a growing crop, and we also recognise its scenic value in a national park. Wordsworth, it could be said, thought of the idea of national parks when he wrote his *Guide to the Lakes*. He wanted the Lake District preserved and he said: 'In this wish the author will be joined by persons of pure taste throughout the whole island, who by their visits (often repeated) to the Lakes in the North of England, testify that they deem the district a sort of national property, in which every man has a right and interest who has an eye to perceive and a heart to enjoy.'

When I first perceived and enjoyed this view I had no idea that I would become the National Park's first warden. Nor could I imagine the experiences it would bring to me: the pleasures and tragedies, the excitement and hilarity, the exhilaration and the hardship, and – oh yes, my Neolithic friend – the frustrations, for I too could make mistakes. And you, I am sure, between your endless chipping here would enjoy the austere beauty of the vista of mountain tops, and the moving air, the clean air of the summits on

14

such a day as this, or the sharp-biting purifying winds of winter. After the day's work you, I am sure, would put down your granite hammer and retreat down to some neck of the woods you called home. Down to the wooden walls of the forest. That's for me too.

———————

'Applications
are invited'

The Lake District National Park office was inundated with inquiries about the newly advertised post of National Park Warden. So we were told. That offered me very little hope but I would try hard. I already knew quite a bit about the setting up of Britain's ten national parks but I wanted to have all the facts right so I visited the library and did some background reading. National Parks in Britain are rather different to those in other countries. They aim to fulfil much the same purpose – the conservation of natural beauty; but in England designation as a national park does not mean that there is national ownership of the land. The setting up of national parks in countries where there were vast areas of wilderness was comparatively simple. It was just a matter of drawing a boundary on a map and declaring that all within it should belong to the nation. After all, the only inhabitants were a few Indians and some pioneers in racoon-skin caps. In Britain the natives are far more savage than that. No great areas of land could be taken from them. Most of the land was under agricultural use anyway. However a line might be drawn on the map around an area of special 'natural' beauty, and designated as a National

Park, subject to stringent Planning Control. Preservation is the first duty; the second is to make sure that the public can enjoy the National Park as freely and responsibly as possible. 'It is because this is a densely populated and highly industrialised country,' said the Hobhouse Committee which made recommendations in 1947 on National Parks, 'that people need the refreshment which is obtainable from the beauty and quietness of unspoilt country.'

When Wordsworth suggested the Lake District's preservation, he was expressing the nineteenth century's growing international concern at the widespread selfish destruction of wilderness and natural landscape. But if the conception of national parks in Britain is old, their inception did not occur until 1949, seventy-seven years after the world's first national park was established at Yellowstone in the USA. The long history, of exhortation by preservation and recreational groups on the one hand, and the procrastination of successive governments on the other, is a dismal one.

I purposely sought and read the Lake District National Park Board's minutes from the park's designation since 1952. I discovered why members concluded that a warden was needed and the duties they thought might be required of him. I filled in the application form very carefully bearing this in mind, and I spent a good deal of time on the last page under the heading: 'Any other details which the applicant may care to mention'.

After a long wait, so long that hope had completely evaporated, there was the shock. I was to be interviewed. Another welcome gap gave me the opportunity of writing down the questions which I thought were likely to be asked, and time to sort out the answers in my mind. I felt uneasy about being asked how well I knew the Lake District. I would have to be frank and admit that I knew very little. The National Park covered 866 square miles. To know it

17

well would take more than one lifetime.

I was depressed when I saw the standard of some of the opposition on interview day, seated in the waiting room at County Hall. I knew some of them. They looked relaxed. I felt as if I were dressed up like the dog's dinner. The tweed suit I was wearing had been given to me. I felt it was too loud when I had a look at myself in the mirror in the washroom. I looked like a comedian. Perhaps I should start the interview with 'A funny thing happened to me on the way to County Hall...' Well, I had nothing to lose. I would go in smiling. When my name was called I was frightened to find that I was facing a whole committee round a long table in the interview room. The chairman was in a throne at the head. It was a set piece like 'When did you last see your father?' But when I answered the first question I was suddenly aware that they were all smiling encouragement. I then relaxed completely when I found I was being asked precisely what I had anticipated. It seemed a very long interview and I left in a daze, thanking everyone, and heading for the wrong door.

'You can call back at four-thirty if you wish,' said the pretty young lady at reception as she handed me a form to claim expenses. 'The decision will have been made by then.' She obviously did not reckon much for my chances; she was not even looking at me, but was smiling at a handsome looking giant of a new interviewee who had just come in.

Hours later I had just arrived home after a day's work when the first telephone call came. It was from a national newspaper. How did I feel about being selected from five hundred applicants for such a challenging job? I was so stunned that I have no idea what I told the man, but as soon as I hung up on him the telephone rang again and the chairman of the committee congratulated me and told me that a letter had been sent offering me the post. What had happened to the opposition? It was a year or so later when the late Lady Lowther, a member of the committee (and also a volunteer warden), confided, 'I voted for you because you were the only man without a beard.' It was obviously a razor-edge decision.

The newspaper reports the next day were slightly hilarious. One headline was 'Lakeland's man of steel'. In fact all my friends knew that any qualities I might possess were strictly non-ferrous. 'Lakeland's man of stiff cardboard'? Perhaps not. 'Lakeland's man of rather strong tin'?

On 1 September I picked up the second-hand Land Rover and visited County Hall. My superior explained very vaguely what I might do, and very definitely what I should not do in my new job. The medical officer listened to my heart, read my medical history and told me that I would likely live to old age if I took care. And a cynical administration officer said he had read my qualifications, my job description and conditions of service, and told me that he would give me six months after which my resignation or complete collapse was certain. Bewildered, I was not confident enough to accept his wager.

September was a good time to start. There was, as Longfellow said, 'that nameless splendor everywhere, that wild exhilaration in the air'. The Lake District took on a new splendour and I was certainly exhilarated. But, yes, I felt very apprehensive and very inadequate too.

Elterwater Common

I was about to set off by Land Rover on my first patrol when I found myself facing a contingent of cronies at my gate who in a mock-solemn ceremony presented me with an ornate litter spike made at the shipyard at Barrow in Furness (and without doubt skilfully smuggled out). I accepted the gift with dignity and a suitable speech and drove off to the misty blue hills.

To Langdale, where else? Langdale draws its enthusiasts like no other valley. It is a place for active enjoyment though. You cannot passively soak in atmosphere in Langdale. It is a valley girt with steep fells and crags – the Pikes, Crinkle Crags, Bowfell; its unique natural architecture makes it familiar to many thousands of Lakeland enthusiasts – even if many only see it from afar. It is not typically English landscape. It is not wold, or down, or moor. It is more barbarous and uncompromising. Not Celtic either; there are not the vast brooding spaces familiar to the Highlander. Nordic? It is no accident that so many of the Lake District place names have Norse origins, for the district was settled by Norsemen from Ireland and the Isle of Man a thousand years ago. They settled peaceably. Many were Christians and they made the central mountainous area their own, leaving the surrounding plains to the Angles. So villages have Norse names. I once had a Norwegian student hitch-hiker who told me which Lake District village names could be found in Norway. Passing a signpost to Scarness he exclaimed, 'I was born in Scarness!' The Lake District hills are fells (from the Norse *fjall*), streams are becks (Norse *bekkr*), waterfalls are forces (Norse *foss*), small mountain lakes are tarns (Norse *tjorn*).

To me the moving evidence for the peaceful coexistence between Norse and Angle is the close proximity in date and location of two fine stone crosses, beautifully preserved: the Angle cross at Irton churchyard, and only a few miles to the north-west the Viking cross at Gosforth. The latter is the more exciting as it shows that the Vikings were relatively new to the Christian faith. On one side of the slender cross, in Norse mythology, is depicted the conquest of evil by good, and on the other side the Christian equivalent. But the Angles and the Norsemen were not competing for the same land. Langdale was not a place for ox-ploughs.

Langdale is a magnet for the active holiday-maker, offering exciting space for tramping escapees from urban claustrophobia, challenging crag walls for climbers, cash to the hoteliers, and a bemusing mixture of wonder and aggravation to the fell farmers. Bank Holidays in the first year of my appointment brought general chaos and anarchy. Tents were scattered along the commons and in any field not cleared by the farmers all the way from Elterwater at the valley's foot to the great green floor of Mickleden at its head. On my appointment Elterwater Common was a problem area, covered with tents in the holiday season, with no drinking water and no sanitation. Camping there was illegal, but there was nobody to stop it. In the village of Elterwater the inhabitants were plagued with requests for

21

water; outdoor lavatories were used by campers, indeed people even queued for them. One inhabitant who drew his water from an outside tap in his yard was told by queueing campers to 'get in line and wait your turn'. Housewives found their clothes-lines dressed overall with campers' washing. The pubs were overcrowded and there were rowdy scenes after closing time.

'It's just like t' wild west,' one villager told me. He was leaning on his drystone garden wall, smoking his pipe and his face flushed with indignation as he told his tale. 'I've known this valley for sixty year but nowt like this 'as 'appened afore. You could al's be sure of quiet neets. You could leave your door unlocked and nowt ivver went missin'. Now you even have to lock t' shed door. They'll pinch your coal for camp fires, tak vegetable out o' t' garden, eggs out of t' hen-hoose – aye hens as well. And what the 'ell can one policeman do? They won't send any extra, they're wanted for traffic duty in Carlisle. T' lad does his best.'

I called on 't' lad'. He was in his shirt sleeves and up to his elbows in grease outside the police house in the next village, fitting a dynamo into his car. He apologised for not shaking hands and said that he was glad to see me.

'You've timed your start right, for September,' he grinned. 'The excitement's over more or less till next Easter. Then God help you! Easter's the worst. It's not as bad as a lot of folk make out, but it's bad enough. Most of the campers are all right. It's just a bad minority. Some of them are regulars and known to us. Given the chance next year with some backing and we'll hit 'em hard and that'll make a difference.'

I walked around Elterwater Common and was sickened by the piles of litter and rubbish. Some of it was half-hidden in the bracken, some dropped in the drainage channels;

22

there were also, alas, signs of dumping from the villagers – food cans, milk bottles, cartons, newspapers, bed frames, wet mattresses. There was scorched ground and the remains of camp fires. Half-burnt fence posts showed one source of fuel. I was appalled and vowed that a clean-up would be one of my first jobs.

The next weekend I was joined by a schoolmaster friend who had rustled up some of his teenage pupils as volunteers. There were twelve in all – eight boys and four girls. Issued with plastic bags, none of them wasted any time. First we collected all the combustible rubbish to put in one pile and soon got a fire going. Onto this went paper, plastic sheets, the remains of other fires, items of clothing, old boots, shoes, mattresses, torn sleeping bags and remnants of tents. I was soon to discover that if you are using a volunteer work party, it is a good idea to light a bonfire. It becomes the focal point for the work area. In rainy weather it is a morale booster, and if someone needs a break from heavy work – he can stoke the fire. However, one of the boys soon discovered that if he threw aerosol cans on the fire impressive explosions took place. So a leader must check the enthusiasm of his volunteers.

We were going to take the non-combustible litter to the dump, but one of the boys was keen to dig a hole. We later found that this lad was an addicted hole-digger. Given a mattock and a spade and you could forget all about him. Later we were all sat down for lunch and someone asked, 'Where's Joggs?' A search party eventually found him when they saw a spade materialising out of the ground scattering soil at a regular rhythm. He was down at the bottom of the hole having a great time. We had to haul him out.

By dropping all the rubbish in the hole and compacting it at intervals with the sledge hammer, we gradually disposed of the mess. We threw in the ashes from the fire, covering

23

them with soil; then the grass sods were put back and trampled down. We walked about the common and surveyed our handywork. After a full day we were tired and dirty, but it was satisfying to see the difference. We had made a start, the first of many of those back-breaking and sometimes near heart-breaking, clean-up jobs. If I was to launch a campaign to teach respect for the countryside, I had to start by making it look respectable.

My friend from the village looked at what we had done, took out his pipe, spat, and said, 'You'll find you've wasted your time. It'll be as bad in a week when t' next visitor season starts.'

Mist

September. A season of mists and mellow fruitfulness. Mists? Mists mean confusion and getting lost. In 1961 I was leading a party of young people in a walk in Grizedale Forest and got lost. I remember it well. So do others.

'Remember me?' asked a vicar's wife I met walking with her children at Back o' Skiddaw. 'I was in your party of cadets when you got us lost in Grizedale Forest.'

Alas, I will never live it down. It was the mist and my arrogant assumption that I could never ever again get lost in a forest. I had only, I thought, to walk through the place once and I would recognise individual trees again, groups of trees, stands of trees, the shape of trees leaning from the wind, leaning into light. Regimented lines of conifers? Here are twelve-year-old Sitka spruces, followed by twenty-year old European larch, some of them malformed through canker, then a scattering of silver firs among twenty-year old Norway spruce, a fire break, a great tilted outcrop of Silurian slate, then Norways as far as the eye can see long past their Christmas tree usefulness. There is always something to catch the eye and interest in Grizedale. Nothing dull and repetitive really if you look carefully. And if you

25

enjoy what you see you do not forget. It is far easier for me to get lost in a city than in a forest. Groups of trees are more familiar and distinctive to me than buildings and streets which do not conform to nature's pattern. I enjoy looking at good buildings, but in a week's stay in the beautiful city of Bath I was lost more times than I was lost in the Lake District forests in years.

Having said that, there was this mist in Grizedale Forest that hung clammily over everything, distorting distance and disguising familiar views. An occasional brief glance at a compass, which I should have had in my pocket, would have saved the situation, but I was hopelessly over-confident and had left it at home. We set out from the wild-life museum at Grizedale for Brantwood, once the home of John Ruskin but now a hostel. It was a straightforward journey that I had made several times before. The first part was easy enough but after that I was so busy chatting enthusiastically to my charges and looking at mosses, liverworts, plants, fungi, and deer tracks, that I lost track of where we were going. Everything was unfamiliar. I told myself that it was a trick of the mist and that I was on the right route. But the forest track seemed to be too long, and the path I should have seen leaving it on the right did not appear although I was constantly looking for it. At last my slight concern was noticed and the dozen youngsters were beginning to get amused. Could it really be possible that their experienced leader who lived and breathed the countryside was lost? He was soon convinced that he was.

When there is no wind, no sound to guide you and visibility is obscured, without a compass there is little one can do. 'The moss always grows on the north side of a tree' we were once told as boy scouts. Quite correct. But moss grows in shade, so that in a wood that means it grows south-west and east as well. 'Exposed trees grow away from

26

the prevailing wind.' That is true too, but in the middle of a dense forest there are no exposed trees. I had nothing to go on but instinct – and that is untrustworthy indeed. If I had been alone I would have enjoyed the experience of getting lost. But I was a guide.

We were, I thought, making too much height. Somehow we had missed the path turn-off. To strike off to the right was unthinkable. The growth was far too low and dense. Presently we came to a strange forest track going off to the right. That should not have been there at all. It was useless looking at the map. It did not show the majority of the forest extraction roads and tracks; bulldozers move more quickly than map makers. Well, it was no use making more height; the right-hand track seemed to be going down and in the direction I felt we ought to go.

I was now most definitely in unknown territory and going through high Norway spruces. To make matters worse the track suddenly gave out and we were walking on what appeared to be a deer path. The thing to do, I thought, apart from putting on an act of cheerful confidence, was to keep descending and, unless we had turned full circle, which God forbid, we would be certain to come down to the road on the east side of Coniston Water. Then even the deer path gave out and I chose a line relatively free of trees where a long flush was far too boggy to support them. We were squelching down then, ankle deep in peaty bog.

'Do you think we will find our way to Brantwood before dinner?' asked an anxious teenage girl. (It is a fallacy that males get hungrier than females.)

'Of course!'

'The mist is getting thicker,' said someone else.

'That's because we're getting nearer to the lake,' I said, and (with more hope than confidence), 'We'll soon be on

27

terra firma.'

Then we hit forest trails which seemed to go in the right direction for a time, but began to mislead. The important thing was to lose height. Eventually I noticed that several of us were looking at watches. I tried to sneak a look at mine.

'Do you know where we are?'

'No,' fingers crossed, 'But we're going in the right direction.'

Suddenly the trees thinned out and we were at a broken fence. Just below was a wall with a gap in it, and then strangely an open and steeply descending moor. There was however, glory be, a path, and at one soft spot I actually found the print of a human foot. It was as exciting a discovery as Robinson Crusoe's. The path eventually led onto a track between drystone walls, but the contours had levelled out and that was worrying. Now I was really anxious. If we had indeed done a full circle and were heading back into the Grizedale valley it would mean getting transport to Brantwood and I would never be trusted again. I would, I feared, have to emigrate, the scandal would be too much. The track descended, however, by a ruined hog-house and other tracks joined ours. I pushed everyone on faster and soon we were at a gate, through it and onto a tarmac road. Now where were we? I strained my eyes beyond the wall on the far side of the road, and with deep gratitude noticed that beyond the fringe of trees there was light space and, asking everyone to keep quiet, I heard the lapping of lake water.

'We're too far south,' I said, 'but all we have to do is to walk right along this road and we'll be at Brantwood in no time.'

'No time' in fact was a little less than one hour and we had time to do little more than throw off our boots before the dinner gong.

28

I was, of course, ribbed unmercifully and cheekily. I tried to convince the youngsters that I had deliberately got them lost to see how they behaved under stress. They were quite unreasonably incredulous.

Mists on the mountains lead to even greater confusion, as landmarks are farther apart and invariably obscured. The uninitiated continue to stride out when the mist suddenly descends, confident that they can continue on the right route. They have just seen the path in front reaching on as clear as can be. It is still there at their feet and all they have to do is to keep on it. But mist on the hill has the strange effect of distorting time too. Old folk-tales of walkers getting lost in the mountain mist and finding themselves in another age, or returning, like Rip Van Winkle, and finding themselves a hundred years on, may well have their origins in the strange confusion that one has in the mountain mist. The over-confident go on with gradually growing apprehension, wondering why they have not reached the cairn they saw before the mist's descent. A friend of mine in a very wet mist was disturbed that he had not reached the small lake of Stickle Tarn long after he thought he should, so he paused to dig into his pocket for another look at his compass, then noticed that he was standing over his ankles in the water.

Then the uninitiated, gradually losing confidence, suddenly find that the path forks, which they did not at all expect, and decisions have to be made. If they have a compass it might well be too late to use it with accuracy as they have already wandered off their correct line. The time to get out the compass is just as the mist is descending, to take a quick bearing of the visible destination, compute the time necesary to reach it, and check the time with a watch. Compass in hand, it is only necessary to occasionally check the line is correct.

I remember a Saturday in another September on the path

along the Blea Rigg heading for Grasmere. It was a bright mild day to begin with, but the forecast of low cloud by mid-morning was correct. The fine start had tempted hundreds of walkers on the fells. I was walking back from Langdale. In fine weather this is a very pleasant walk, with airy views over the Langdale valley if you keep to the higher path. But it is notoriously easy to lose oneself there in mist as there are no landmarks of note. This day when the mist came I worked out a bearing for Easedale Tarn on the compass and slung it round my neck on its cord for easy reference. Then I heard an argument below me between a male and a female.

'It's this way I tell you!'

'Good grief, woman, I know this path! We go down to our right.'

The fell mists cause many arguments between long bosom friends – even newly-weds. Indeed, I suspect that a honeymoon walk into the mist has started thousands of marriages off down the slippery slope (figuratively and sometimes literally). I have often seen exhausted wives reduced to tears, and husbands to sulky rages. I have seen two members of the annual Keswick religious convention on a misty Skiddaw disputing in a most ill-tempered and un-Christian manner. Each party in these arguments is convinced that he or she knows the direction and that the other party is utterly stupid. Both might have walked many miles, have become very tired, very edgy, and completely demoralised. Although each is convinced he or she is right however, splitting up is a fearful prospect. Solitude in misty obscurity is terrifying. The stronger personality wins. Heaven help the newly-wed husband if he takes his weary bride against her certain judgement down into the wrong valley to finish with an expensive and late taxi drive back to the hotel.

After a time, I came upon the contenders, and asked them where they were heading. 'Grasmere,' they said. Without commenting on who was right, I suggested that they followed me. It was not long before we heard another argument in the mist in front of us. A family group loomed up this time.

'Which is the Grasmere path?' asked the despairing mum.

'Follow us,' I suggested.

With the responsibility now of new-found charges I sneaked a quick check of my compass and we continued on. Yet another heated discussion below us on our left.

'Where are you for?' I called through the murk.

'Grasmere.'

'Come this way.'

We waited. A group of elderly walkers, equipped for a stroll in some urban park, joined us.

'Follow us.'

We continued. I looked back. The mist was so thick that there was no way of making sure if we were all together. I knew they were there by the animated discussions and, when the path degenerated into oozy bog, by their cries of discomfort and disgust. There were calls to right and left too, and directions shouted: 'This way!' Within half an hour the noise behind seemed to have grown mysteriously in volume and the mist began to thin. The curtain was pulled away and there was Easedale Tarn. I walked on and shortly afterwards looked back as my party also broke through the mist. It was an astonishing sight. I had collected quite a crocodile of walkers of all descriptions. And at the back, (I rubbed my eyes) like jolly penguins, were three elderly nuns!

I waited for them. They were in their habits, wearing low shoes covered in brown ooze; they were laughing with enjoyment. 'Where have you been?' I asked. They told me that they had not the slightest notion. It started as a fine day and they had thought it would be rather nice to walk up on the hills. Faith indeed.

Looking through the mountain-rescue records, it is remarkable how religious people so often go astray in the earthly sense if not in the spiritual. Alas, faith needs to be supplemented with a map and compass in the mists. On a search one fearfully cold night for a priest with a party of children, my team eventually found them crouched in an exposed position on the mountain and suffering from the first stages of hypothermia.

'I knew you would come,' the priest told us, 'for we all sat down and prayed.'

Some years earlier a night search was mounted for a lone priest, a shepherd who had not returned to his fold. The experienced rescue team leader, after an honest day's hard work, had been in a very strenuous search of the bleak and foggy mountain. Having eventually found the priest he was told, 'I prayed, and I knew that God would help me.' The grimly resigned and weary team leader handed over a flask of hot coffee, sighed, and said, 'Yes. Well. I don't know how God feels, but *I'm* bloody tired.'

Fungi

The October woods have the smell of autumn. How can one begin to describe it? Coming down from the clear sterile air of the fell and facing the aromatic impact of the autumn woods is to me an exciting, physical shock. It is the smell of moist lying leaves, of brown humus, of dead wood. But the real tangy spicy smell, the peppery yeasty smell, comes from the moulds that colonise the woods and come into their own, for autumn is the fungi's spring time. All the year the billions of spores have lain to await their day. Then in the mild humidity their thread-like growth, the hyphae, spreads rapidly in the darkness beneath the leaf litter, under the bark of dead wood, through the rich black topsoil, under the tree roots. The smouldering dark embers have awaited their turn to share in the awesome fecundity of the forest and burn into their season. The fruiting heads in their amazing variety burst overnight into the air, brown, red, orange, yellow, purple, olive and sooty black. The speed of their appearance has long bred a sort of superstitious awe, and this and their unjustified overall deadly reputation as poisoners cause a common destructive reaction. But they do not deserve to be despised. They are a vital part of the great web of life. Only one species of toadstool in Britain, the death cap, *Amanita phalloides*, is deadly poisonous; some are dangerous, some are emetics, some cause hallucinations; but many are edible, and some are very good.

Their function is fascinating. They are plants incapable of photosynthesis and so cannot manufacture their own food from sunlight and air as normal plants do. They must rely on the absorption of food from the organic matter of their host. So they are parasitic, and many of the species hasten the process of decay. But many species live in a mutually vital association with other plants. The majority of the orchids depend upon this 'mycorrhizal' association and forest trees also owe their healthy growth to the presence of fungi about their roots. Fungi also help to break down leaves and woodland floor litter into productive humus.

One can understand the human repugnance for these parasites; but even the parasitic fungi serve humanity. The housewife obviously hates to find her jam preserves, or her potted meats, covered by a woolly growth. That particular fungus produces vast quantities of spores which move everywhere in the air. It is the curse of scientists trying to work in sterile laboratories. One day in 1928 a scientist discovered to his annoyance that one of his cultures of the bacterium *Staphylococcus aureas* in his laboratory was contaminated by the same fungus and to his surprise found that it was effectively destroying the bacterium. The scientist was Alexander Fleming and the fungus was penicillium. So the despair of housewife and scientist became the revolutionary destroyer of infection, the life-saver penicillin.

But some fungi do costly damage. Some species, common in woodlands, cause spectacular destruction to buildings. The chief culprit is *Serpula lacrymans* – dry-rot. Fungi cannot flourish without moisture, but once established dry-rot fungus can spread quickly into dry woodwork; its long hyphae, its thrusting filaments, which can grow out for several metres across concrete or brickwork into sound wood, are able to carry enough water to live on. To go into a building in an advanced stage of decay, with the sinister fruiting bodies breaking out in unlikely places, spreading spores to start new infections, and with the floor crumbling under your feet, is a horrible experience. I inspected a long-abandoned social club building which the National Park was considering turning into a workshop. As soon as I entered from the bright sunlight of the street I felt that I was in some sort of house of horrors. First there was the strong humid smell which was stuffy and almost overpowering. Then I noticed the peculiar angles of the wooden floor. There was a closed venetian blind at a window. I pulled the cord to open it. It fell with a crash and raised a choking dust which set me sneezing violently. Then I noticed in the improved light the fruit bodies and great yellow areas ringed with swollen edges of white – everywhere. It was even covering the metal taps on the sink, the sides of the heating stove. It completely enveloped the green-baize cloth on the table. The floor felt dead under my feet. I thrust one foot down and it went clean through a board. I could not get out into the bright sunlight quickly enough.

Another which causes a great deal of costly damage to commercial forestry is the honey fungus, *Armillaria mellea*, for it creeps along under the forest floor and enters and destroys live trees. Expensive attempts are made to control the fungus, but it is extremely resilient. New outbreaks can only become established in dead wood. So after felling, the tree stumps are often treated with a fungicide. But if the fungus is already in the ground little can be done to prevent the insidious spreading invasion by the rhizomorph, the root-like mycelium whose long black 'bootlace' strands can force their way into live tree roots and bark.

Actually the honey fungus has for centuries been regarded with suspicious awe. There is a peculiar reason. Years ago on a summer evening I had gathered a large quantity of dead oak wood which had been piled on the ground at the edge of the nearby forest after felling. The branches were of such a thickness that they could be cut by one or two blows of a felling axe rather than by sawing. So I spent a busy few hours cutting up hearth-size lengths. Later that evening I walked in the darkness past the chopping block which I had been using. As I approached I became aware of a weird green light. Then I saw that the whole of the floor area around the block was lit by the light of luminous fragments of wood. I picked up the glowing pieces and with one of them I could read the time on my watch. I scooped up chips by the handful and poured them in a luminous waterfall onto the ground. I carried some into the darkness of my home and they glowed on the kitchen table. The luminous wood was almost certainly permeated with the mycelium of honey fungus, which becomes luminous within a certain temperature range.

Some other fungi have the same strange property. Dr John Ramsbottom, a leading British authority on fungi, records a similar experience. Troops digging trenches at Arnheim in October 1944 were surprised to find the trenches shining with luminous wood. Tree roots glowed when they were split open. A specimen was later sent to Dr Ramsbottom who identified the mycelium of honey fungus.

The phenomenon is familiar to foresters, and miners sometimes see it in the timbers deep underground. Centuries ago a tree affected by honey fungus with some parts glowing in the dark would be regarded as magic. A glowing wand taken from it could easily be believed to have special powers.

To me some fungi are as beautiful as flowering plants. The obvious one to excite the eye is the fly agaric, *Amanita muscaria*. This is the toadstool of red and white portrayed in children's books, the home of elves and pixies. Its odd name arises from the reports that it was of old used as an insecticide. The white spots are the broken remnants of the veil which encloses the juvenile stage of the fruiting body. The fly agaric is dangerous if eaten, but in very small quantities it has long been known for its powers of intoxication. In certain parts of Eastern Europe it is added to alcoholic drinks to increase their effect. It has been suggested too that the Viking raiders used the drug to produce a suitable state of frenzy before attack. The fungus is not a parasite; on the contrary, it lives in mycorrhizal association with pines and birches, and it must have marched with these first colonisers, following the retreat of the ice-age glaciers.

I have other favourites. The bright glowing orange peel fungus, *Aleuria aurantia*, appears on forest tracks; it almost seems to glow with an inner light. The parasol mushroom, *Macrolepiota procera*, looks like a pretty fabric-covered parasol, but the delicious nutty flavour is its great attraction for me. I also search the floor of October woods for the bright yellow chanterelle, another culinary delight. It comes sometimes plentifully after a lot of rain and it benefits the beech trees among whose roots it grows. One not at all edible, but to me strangely fascinating, is the bracket fungus which grows on birch trees. This is the tough 'razor strop' fungus, *Piptoporus betulinus*. The fungus, plucked from a trunk, is like tough thick leather and feels indestructible. If it could take nails it could probably make good boot soles. There is hardly a dying birch in my woods unaffected by this parasite and whether the fungus

37

came to affect the dead wood, or whether it caused the tree's deaths is not known. Pure birch woods are sometimes rather dangerous to an unwary explorer. Brushing against what looks like sound trunks (as the silver bark is immune to rot) can sometimes bring infected trunks and their high branches down upon your head. Another attractive, but poisonous, fungus is sulphur tuft, *Hypholoma fasciculare*, which grows in great yellow clumps on dead wood – particularly on an old log by my front gate regularly each autumn.

Fungi of all kinds produce spores in enormous quantities. They have an uncomfortable effect on me. When I visited hospital to have tests to discover the cause of my sometimes tormenting hay fever, I was eventually told that I had an allergy to some pollens, but particularly to spores. I went to see my doctor to see if he could give me something one day to alleviate my symptoms. The waiting room overlooked the churchyard like all good country practices; but the surgery overlooked many acres of oak and ash. The doctor then was a bluff countryman looking forward to imminent retirement to spend all his time fishing. He had a reputation for speaking his mind. Whenever I went to see him he always talked first about the season, the birds, the deer, quizzed me about the doings of the National Park, railed about the damage being done by some land owners, particularly the Forestry Commission, and eventually got round to asking what on earth I was doing in his surgery as I looked as fit as a fiddle and he had quite enough to do caring for sick people. I told him and he shook his head.

'Want a certain cure?' he snapped.

'Yes please,' I told him.

He nodded to the window. 'Get out of your wet woods. Clear off and live in Manchester or Liverpool.'

It was sound advice. What he was saying in his way was

'Be grateful and suffer in silence.'

The Lecture Season

Winter is the season for evening lectures. I can look back at hundreds of talks I have given to schools, youth groups, various clubs, Workers' Education classes, extra-mural courses, parish meetings, church groups, Rotary, and of course Women's Institutes. The Women's Institute is the best thing that ever happened to country villages in the last century. I cannot remember ever regretting talking to a Women's Institute, but if you get known in the area you can have far too many requests to speak. I once attended a short course on 'public speaking and presenting a lecture'. It was very good and the advice was sound. 'You should attend at the lecture room well in advance of the fixed time,' said the tutor, 'to erect your screen and projector and to try it out.' He wondered why so many of us were smiling at this. If it were only that easy.

You bolt down a meal, throw projector, slides, screen, stand, and notes into your vehicle and go out into the pitch black night, possible through rain, fog, or snow, for what could be a long drive. You may need to stop once or twice when getting near the village to consult your map and with luck you are in the unlit village looking for the Institute some twenty minutes before your time. Probably you mistakenly believe that the hall with all the cars parked outside is the Institute. You unload part of your gear, stagger in the rain to the door, then find it is a meeting of the badminton club, or the parochial church council in discussion – and you may poke your head round the door at a pregnant moment. However, you find the right spot. You will have been given a time when you might be expected to talk, in which case you usually arrive during the business meeting when they are asking for volunteers to supply pies, cakes, and biscuits for the forthcoming area gathering. Sometimes you are given the time when the meeting starts, in which case you arrive just before they all stand up to sing 'Jerusalem', accompanied by an out-of-tune piano, which is preferable to the distorted tones of the gramophone record. Anyhow you certainly have no time to set up long before you start. It is, in fact, dangerous to do so as projectors are expensive and easily knocked over.

Eventually, however, you are introduced and everyone waits expectantly while you erect the screen, stand, and projector in three minutes flat – if you are lucky. The screen is an enemy, a familiar monster I have never mastered. In the process of unfolding I usually manage to trap my fingers and have to struggle before the fascinated audience to transform a scream of agony to a mere grimace. Having been stood up and extended, the contraption often bangs down shut with a noise like a rifle-shot, to the terror of the more timid who were not watching, or it refuses to extend to its proper height. The folding stand with detachable legs is another hazard never to be erected within earshot of the vicar's wife. The projector is set up, the extension lead is run out – and you find that the electric plug is of the round-pin type which were never fitted after 1950 and are still now only to be seen in remote village institutes. I used to carry one of those plugs, which, by the turn of a screw, and a bit of a shake (with your tongue held firmly to the right of your mouth) produced any type of archaic plug pin pattern. I gave it up after it started to produce confused patterns of various combinations, and one embarrassing evening when the result was an interesting display of pyrotechnics which blew all the hall's main fuses. I find it easier now to carry a screwdriver and borrow a plug off the Institute's vacuum cleaner. But it all takes time and the fact that you are being watched is unnerving. At last you switch the projector on; there is a moment of panic until you find that the plug switch is not on. Sometimes the bulb blows instantly because there is something wrong with the voltage. But that does not deter. Experience has taught me to carry three spares. (On one night two bulbs went in rapid succession.)

All should go well, though I remember with horror the nights when I dropped the magazine of slides and had to hurriedly throw them back in some semblance of order. Slides which then appeared upside down were quickly flicked through. If they were human figures I made some comment about Australian visitors. A deer which appeared to be walking up a vertical crag was passed off with a remark about the animal's ability to adapt to its environment.

Having successfully delivered the talk, you must dismantle equipment while trays of teas and buns are being circulated. This is a hazardous business. But then there is the ultimate horror, for as guest speaker you are required to judge the evening's competition. The most terrifying one was an Easter bonnet competition which I try hard to forget. But sometimes it is the most apt verse, or holiday snaps, or anti-litter posters, or 'useful articles of yesteryear', or small floral arrangements – or absolutely anything.

Whatever happens you must take great care not to give the first prize to the Institute's unpopular member, who is probably an arts graduate, wins all the competitions, and gives herself airs. You can always tell if you inadvertantly pick hers out by the very feeble hand-clapping, but then you will be too late. You can, by picking out the efforts of the unpopular as winner, start a contention which will rock the Institute to its foundations and lead to resignations from office, a reshuffle of the hierarchy, or it may even start off a chain reaction affecting all the village population. So it is well to take care. A friend of mine who also does the institute circuits tells me that he invariably picks out the least attractive entry. He says it does the least harm and encourages the strugglers.

The tea, cakes and sandwiches are always excellent if you are allowed to enjoy them because this is when ladies come to you to ask questions, or to recount to you their fell-walking experiences, or to tell you that they have a nephew who would love to be a national park warden and to ask how he should work towards it. It is not always easy to answer when chewing crumbly scones or cream sponges.

Some of the engagements stick in my memory. There was a Lancashire Institute more miles away than I normally travel, but the invitation was very persuasive and they said it was their guest-night so members from other Institutes would be present. I arrived somewhat weary after the longish drive, pulled into the village square and stepped out to reconnoitre. I could see that it was a beautiful well-kept tidy village even by moonlight and then I heard it – the great chorus of 'Jerusalem' booming out enthusiastically and making the windows rattle. I have never heard the like since. The parish room was packed solid and – a nice touch this – at the end I was obliged to take my refreshments on the stage with the president, and no one was allowed to speak to me until I had finished.

Then there was the equally pretty Cumbrian village. We had arrived here very early with the intention of having light refreshments first at the one village inn which was noted for its hospitality. But the landlord told us that the inn only served dinners. I told him that we had not the time to sit to dinner and he shrugged his regrets. We drove off in disgust to the next village which was even more picturesque than the first, and by good fortune arrived at the village green at the same time as a mobile fish-and-chip shop. When I took my place at last in the village hall the president asked, 'Didn't I see you in the village earlier?' I told her that we had arrived early to refresh ourselves at the pub but had not been served. The president was a large lady and there came a light of battle in her eyes that would make the bravest man tremble. She stalked out of the room and across the road to the pub. I would not have been in the landlord's shoes for anything. In fact, the pub was up for sale shortly afterwards.

There have been moments of horror. I was sitting on the high stage behind the table with the lady officers awaiting my cue, when I happened to look down and noticed my lower shirt in full view. I realised to my panic that my trousers were unfastened. I assumed an air of indifference while at the same time making a surreptitious attempt to zip up. The zip was broken. The president was speaking. I touched the sleeve of the secretary and asked her if I could make a temporary escape and have the loan of some safety pins. She asked why and I had to explain my trouble. She covered a smile with her hand, whispered wickedly, 'Oh dear. Shall I announce it?' But, bless her, she scribbled a note and passed it to the president. 'Speak for five minutes while speaker makes temporary escape.' In the best British tradition the president accepted the instruction without query. The secretary nodded to a door behind the stage while struggling to retain her composure. 'First aid box on the kitchen wall.' I turned quickly round in my chair and made my escape and repairs.

On one occasion I was making an expressive gesture with my right hand and knocked a jug of water over the treasurer's account book, instantly putting the account in debit. And once when taking my refreshments after my talk, a pickled onion which had been given to me with a portion of meat pie evaded my fork and projected itself onto the president's chair where it was promptly sat upon by the elegant functionary.

I have also arrived with the wrong slides for the talk. But the error was never as bad as that suffered by a GP who was giving a talk on first aid, roused everyone's interest with his preamble, then switched on the projector to show slides – of his sister's wedding.

One of the most testing engagements was to address a group of blind and visually handicapped people on 'The Lake District as a National Park'. I had to think about it and decided that all I could do was to take along some lumps of the National Park for them to handle. I collected samples of rock from all the geological areas, several types of Borrowdale volcanic, granite, Silurian slates, Skiddaw slates, limestone, minerals and new red sandstone. Then I gathered some of the same rocks from various sea shores so that they could feel how the various types had been worn down differently by the action of sea and sand. My audience was fascinated by the symmetrical feel of the crystal samples, and by the flat, perfectly smooth, sea-worn sedimentary rocks. I was then able to describe to them how millions of years of erosion had shaped the landscape in different ways according to the qualities of the rocks. One of the questions repeated as they held the rock was, 'What colour is this?' The rock samples were passed from hand to hand as they sat in a semicircle. We found at the end that two samples had gone missing which was a puzzle until I noticed that one of the guide dogs seemed to have a strangely bulging look about the mouth. On a return visit I talked about the district's early history and took along ancient tools and artifacts borrowed from a museum, but kept a careful eye on that particular dog.

Club dinners I regard as difficult. I dislike after-dinner speeches. At one climbing club dinner all went exceptionally well, however, as the dinner was late owing to an undisclosed crisis in the kitchen. This gave the guests generous drinking time on empty stomachs and some were rather merry, well, to be truthful, most of them. I managed to keep sober and remain so for, when we eventually reached the dinner table, as fast as a drink was poured out for me, and they kept coming fast, it was quaffed by the guest on my right, an ageing and well-respected priest who was drinking from his own glass too. I believe his thefts were done in gay and absent-minded innocence as he conversed away incessantly. When I stood up to speak and cracked my first joke, the whole company broke into a loud roar of laughter. I realised that the atmosphere was decidedly in my favour. I could say nothing wrong. Each opinion received noisy agreement, and even a mild facetious aside was greeted with loud laughter and applause. When I came to the climax of the speech they were practically rolling on the floor and the clapping and table banging was deafening – and the priest on my right was pumping my hand vigorously and breathing my alcohol all over me.

One evening I set off to a Rotary dinner. I allowed myself plenty of time, took some care over my appearance, and drove out into a dark and rainy night. I had a puncture in a front-wheel tyre. First I had a struggle to get the jack in position working by the light of a handlamp lying on a plastic bag in the wet roadside. I had a terrible job to remove the wheel with the feeble little spanner the Land Rover company think is adequate. I then had another struggle fitting the spare as the handlamp battery was giving up and the light was localised and feeble. However, wet and dirty, I threw the offending wheel into the back and continued the journey, now late, as fast as I dare. I noticed that the steering was tricky; and thought that the obvious fault was that the spare was short on air. I arrived dirty, damp, and dishevelled as my audience had just sat down to the meal. However, all went to plan. Then at the end I tackled a friend of mine who was there and was a skilled mechanic and asked if he had a good footpump.

'Bring your Land Rover over to my garage into the light,' he said. 'We'll soon get it right.'

When I did drive into his garage however he looked puzzled, then roared with laughter and I immediately saw why. In the darkness I had managed to put the wheel on inside outward. No wonder I found the steering odd; the wheel stood proud outside the mudguard by inches. After we had put it right I pleaded with him not to mention my daft error to anyone who did not know already as I did not want too many people to know that I was an idiot. He promised but he was laughing. A week or so later I was at a Mountain Rescue advisory panel meeting when the police inspector handing out the agendas gave one to me and said solemnly, without the flicker of an eyelid, 'This is an instruction sheet on how to change Land Rover wheels.'

Radio and television talks give no problems as they are nearly always recorded and every error can be rectified. But once when speaking 'live' on radio I was leaning on a table while expounding about the peaceful countryside when the thing collapsed with a deafening crash. On a television

47

appearance I was using a 'prompter', my script printed on a long ribbon of paper drawn upwards before me on an ingenious machine, when it stuck and left me adlibbing in thinly disguised panic. My first live appearance on commercial television years ago was very nearly a disaster. Three of us had agreed to take part in an evening discussion on conservation, in between pieces of relevant film, and commercial breaks. We met the producer-presenter and his team in the studio at lunchtime to decide how we were to arrange the programme: what questions would be put to whom, how we would reply, and where the pieces of film could be slotted in. There was a lot to discuss and the afternoon seemed to fly. We were all exhausted by the time we went to the canteen for a meal. At this point our producer disappeared. Ten minutes before we were due to start we had been to make-up and were in our seats waiting. No producer. Cameraman and floor manager looked apprehensive and someone was sent off to search. At the due time he was still not with us and there was an extended commercial break. At long last he arrived – but to our horror we saw that he had obviously been drinking. However his notes were put before him and we started. All went well for the first few minutes, but then everything turned sour. His notes were in a mess. He put wrong or irrelevant questions to the wrong people and repeated himself. To avoid embarrassment the cameras kept on us. We managed to hold a three-way discussion without presenter and cued the film in ourselves by saying, 'Haven't we a piece of film to illustrate that point?' All the time the floor manager was writhing about under the cameras with his copy of the now useless notes looking as if he were having a violent fit. During the breaks and films the producer was offered black coffee which he refused angrily, and there was some urgent and heated discussion on how we could continue the next live sequence. Somehow we got through and one of my colleagues summed up at the end superbly. We all then left in a hurry. Strangely everyone who spoke to me about the programme afterwards remarked how good it was. One man went so far as to say that it was the most interesting programme he had seen on the box in years.

One of the most absorbing commissions I have ever had was to assist in what was to be an award-winning radio programme of Norman Nicholson's Lake District poetry, entitled 'A Wall Walks Slowly'. Norman was to read his own poems interspersed with the sounds of the Lake District and the voices of local people. The programme was the brain-child of Desmond Briscoe, director of the BBC's radiophonic workshop. My main task was a challenge. I was given a list of local sounds which they needed to record. This included water – fast running, slow running, waterfalls, lapping on the shore, small streams, splashes – quarry noises, sheep dogs barking, sheep, the mewing of a buzzard and more. The list was formidable. I arranged to meet Desmond, his wife/assistant, Geoffrey, his sound recorder, and Gavin, the local naturalist, in delectable Dunnerdale where I felt sure that we would get all the sounds if we worked from morn to evening. In fact we did it. The only real failure was the buzzard who flew about our heads for a long time but only mewed when the equipment was packed away at lunch-time. But what I enjoyed most of all was learning to listen and appreciate sounds anew. When Geoffrey actually stood in the river shallows at the head of Dunnerdale and lowered his twin microphones almost to water level I thought he was going too far. But he beckoned me into the water and put the earphones over my ears. It was a revelation. Directly close to the microphones water was pouring, spouting, spurting and bubbling over boulders. Each gush came at regular intervals but the rhythms

49

of each was different. The notes were also different but they all fitted together into a regular pattern of time and tune. It was like a piece by Bach.

Ever since I spoke to the visually handicapped, and assisted in the collection of sounds for radio, my appreciation of the feel and the sound of nature has been heightened. A walk up a river can become a music festival. A blackbird's extempore song becomes a serious, masterly recital. I note the difference in the cascade of sound from a birch tree in the wind to the murmuring outburst of an oak. And I can appreciate the sharp-edged crystal feel in a piece of granite, or the silk smooth finish of a sand-scoured volcanic tuff, or the abrasiveness of a hand full of beck gravel, or the coolness and yielding velvet feel of wet moss.

We are part of all we have experienced. Enthusiasm thrives on sharing. Every encounter adds to our secret store. It is there when we want it.

Wind

The trees have spoken all night, dead leaves hissing, limbs creaking and whipping the storming wind until it howled. The rage continued for hours, coming in great waves like breakers on the shore. Sometimes I thought that all would go, trees and house and all. It was, I knew, a north wind with a bit of Icelandic seas in it. The sort of fleeing wind that hurls down from the awful north and slices off the tops of the great sea waves to throw them in a spray like steel bars against the pitching bows of struggling ships. I have feared the north gale and it seems in my haunted dreams that it has followed me to invade the sanctuary of my sheltering trees and to rock the foundations of my piece of earth. Sometimes, in my dreams, I fear that the great sea wastes have followed me to beat against my house; my house is suddenly a small ship and Geordie is shaking my hammock to tell me that I have the middle watch, and I can feel the decks struggling and shuddering to heave out of the hundreds of tons of pounding hammering waters. I drag myself out of this nightmare with a happy smile of relief and turn over. In my mind's eye I can see my bending trees spreading out their arms and hands and throwing the great winds upwards in great eddies above my roof. In one great gust I hear a 'crash!' which wakes me with a start.

Come morning I awake and marvel at the silence. I go out and the trees are standing still and firm and I wonder that they who fought hard all night should be so calm and still, as if nothing has happened. The trees stand like the giants they are, veterans of a thousand campaigns, taking their quiet ease. I expect to see the debris of a battlefield with trunks lying on the ground. But at first sight all looks intact. I remember the cracking noise and see that a large limb has been torn from a Douglas fir and has dropped into a hedge. For the rest there is only a carpet of dead twigs, and dead brown leaves piled in drifts on the lee of the walls. The air has cleared and as the morning lightens I look out beyond the lake to the hills and see that overnight they have been covered by new snow as white as a tablecloth at Sunday teatime.

'Why is wind?' my young son once asked me when we were having a good blow. I tried to answer him. That nothing on the earth stays still, not even the mountains, though sometimes movement is so slow that we cannot see it. That the earth is surrounded by a layer of air that was always in a state of disturbance because it is dragged about by the spinning earth and is pushed into waves by the shape of the land and the differences in temperature. That air piles itself up here, then spills down, flowing and sometimes rushing into hollows there.

'Somewhere,' he mused, 'there must be a very big hole in the air.'

If we are affected by all that we experience, what then of the wind? For the air is always ebbing and flowing and perhaps unknown to us it helps to shape what we are and what we are destined to be. Its effects are subtle, rarely extreme. Climate influences the racial characteristics of a nation and the flowing air makes its mark. Strong winds certainly disturb normal bird and animal activity; deer particularly get restless. Wind pressures surely influence human behaviour patterns too. Gipsies, I was once told, who more than anyone else live in the free air, will work and move unprotected in rain, hail, snow or fog, but they hate a strong wind and are morose and depressed if they have to struggle with one. Farmers, and foresters, and all outdoor workers hate strong winds. It makes everything so difficult and consequences less predictable. And although less work is probably done because of it, one is soon wearied. In a working group, relationships sometimes get strained. It is an old country saying that 'The devil is busy in a high wind'.

Some of the Lake District valleys are notorious for their strange wind eddies. Depending on the direction of the gale, the configuration of the fells brings sudden violent squalls and miniature cyclones. It makes sailing on some of the lakes hazardous to say the least. Several times when I have been in Buttermere in strong winds I have seen whirlwinds pick up waterspouts, and the same turbulence there once twisted the tops off some quite sturdy old lakeshore trees as we watched. But on the fells the effect is even more violent. I have seen stones the size of a fist picked up and bounced about. It is common to see heavy waterfalls, particularly Piers Gill on the side of Scafell Pike, lifted uphill by the great force of an up-draught. I experienced one of these strong up-draughts once when climbing a gully on Dow Crag, Coniston. It seemed as if all the seven winds were channelled into our gully and we were being pushed up as if we were on an escalator of air. We laughed about it afterwards and speculated whether, for safety's sake, we should have rope-belayed from below.

A powerful gale at lower levels can be at near hurricane strength on the fell summits as it sweeps violently upwards from below to join forces with the gales sweeping freely at the higher levels. Watching mountain rescue search dogs trying to pick up air scents in moderately strong winds on summit ridges, one can see the patterns of turbulence. In a strong wind it seems there is a narrow area along an edge which almost is a vacuum. My own dog running along the extreme windward edge of a summit plateau may not pick up the scent of climbers on the cliffs below, but moving back from the edge for some feet she shows an instant reaction. One wintry day from the centre of a plateau she lifted her nose and moved over to the cliff edge to tell me that there were people below. I looked over but saw no one. As she looked down she had obviously lost the scent but her movements told me that she felt she had not made a mistake. I had another look and sure enough there were two climbers eating sandwiches in a shelter they had cut below the snow cornice.

A sudden squall on the mountain top can drop walkers like ninepins and it is rather amazing to me that more accidents have not been caused from wind. I was once thrown bodily down a fell side. I should have known to get down low before the squall hit me for I saw the string of walkers in front of me skittled, but when it did strike me it was like a blast from an explosion. I had turned my back to it and the next thing I knew I was off my feet, hurled forward in the air, then beaten down violently. I started to roll when I hit the ground but was stopped by my rucksack and escaped with a few bruises.

The worst mountain weather is rain with strong winds. It is a killer, for people with inadequate clothing will get wet and rapidly cooled by the wind. Hypothermia comes quickly. It used to be said that the best mountain clothing must 'breathe' to prevent perspiration. No one would be seen in completely impervious jackets before 1965. But one July a man went missing in the Scafell area. The search was continued for four days and it was wet and windy for most of the time. When some mountain rescue personnel had to be sent down off the mountain as they were reaching the first stages of hypothermia, the teams had a rethink, and very soon were re-equipped. Now completely waterproof jackets are standard issue, and outdoor pursuits centres have adopted them too. Best to be warm-wet from perspiration, than cold-wet from wind driven rain.

One can soon be demoralised on the fells by squally weather. Walking becomes a struggle and morale-boosting conversation is impossible. You tend not to take the trouble to pull out your map and assess your position and are inclined to rely on your sense of direction. There is a tendency to move off course into sheltered positions and to walk slightly sideways instead of forward. In such conditions getting lost is easy.

It is an ill wind that blows no good. Wind produces wrack. A work party at Red Tarn below Helvellyn and its ridges found twenty-three hats, five maps, and an assortment of scarves, odd gloves, even spectacles. If I get out of bed after a disturbed night of noisy wind I know that I can collect enough blown dead kindling to last me for a long time. One early morning dash to the seashore in a wind that nearly cut me in half produced enough planks to build several workshop shelf units and a rotten window bottom in my house was replaced by teak.

Tree Planting

When I walk up the lane I can look over the low wall into the wood and see a grove of alder trees set about a wet area around a beck. They wave their branches to the wind way above my head. I planted these trees years ago from seed, first grown in seed boxes made from wooden trays thrown out by a baker, then transplanted into a plot of land, then lifted and planted again where they grow now. Their rate of growth was extraordinary, and the losses almost nil. Yet the seeds were quite tiny.

Although alder is a broadleaved deciduous tree it bears its seed in woody catkins rather like cones. It is a common tree in wet areas. Locally the trees are 'ellers' which is a remarkable survival of its Norse name. Alders can thrive in boggy areas where the roots of most species of trees would 'drown', because the surface roots develop nodules which contain the mycelia of a fungus with the help of which the tree can draw nitrogen from the air. In the Lake District the tree was highly rated for charcoal making, and this was much used in local gunpowder works. It coppices very freely and grows fast. It is easily worked and was once the wood used for making clogs. Alder was once regarded as a valuable herb and Culpeper, the famous seventeenth century astrologer-physician recommended the leaves for burns. He and other herbalists suggested that leaves put on bare feet 'galled by travelling' will greatly refresh them. But I like Culpeper's final suggestion: 'The said leaves gathered while the morning dew is on them, and brought into a chamber troubled with fleas, will gather them thereunto, which being suddenly cast out, will rid the chamber of these troublesome bed-fellows.' I am grateful to have had no opportunity to try the experiment.

Planting alders in swampy land is very hard work. One winter day I planted 400 and it was hard graft. 'Slot' or 'notch' planting is simple if the ground is reasonable. It is a matter of thrusting the planting spade vertically into the ground, with the help of a foot, taking the spade out, turning it ninety degrees and repeating to make an L-shaped cut. With the second thrust you lever up the flap of sod, take a seedling from the bag with your free hand, push it into the gap, remove the spade to allow the flap to close on the seedling's root, then stand firmly on it. Each operation should only take a few seconds. It does not do your back a lot of good eventually, but I was told to keep telling myself, 'I am planting a wood for my children and my children's children.'

That is the theory of it anyway. But the ground is not normally easy ground. If it was it would have been taken into agriculture. A farmer friend once told me that some stones in the soil were better than manure. They were a great aid to fertility. But his land was not in the central Lake District where this kind of 'manure' is in more than plentiful supply. You thrust in your spade. It goes in a few inches and grates. You try a few inches away, it goes in, you turn the spade ninety degrees and push in again, it grates, and you either try somewhere else or see if you can lever the stone out, in which case what you think is a mere pebble proves a good imitation of a foundation stone for a Victorian town hall. You struggle on and you should keep telling yourself, 'I am planting a wood and getting a double hernia for my children and my children's children.' When things are too bad to use a spade then it is necessary to plant with a mattock. On really stony ground swinging a mattock can guarantee to jar every bone in your body. Much of that and even your fingers will find it hard to hold a pint mug afterwards.

But a nice rushy bog for alder planting is something else. Walking on it is bad enough. You try to push in the spade with a wellington boot dragged out of the mire and the mat of moss-covered rush roots sags inwards and remains unbroken. It is like trying to push a putty knife into an inflated rubber tube. So you develop a technique of lifting the spade high and spearing it into the bog to penetrate the top root layer, and then you jump on the spade to get it squelching deeper into the black heavy clinging mire below. This has taken a lot of effort, and you have to turn the blade to make another cut. Your troubles are not over for when you try to lever up the flap, wet suction holds it like a vice. Swing on the spade handle and at first it refuses to move, then it opens with a rush and a slurp, catching you unawares. Do that 400 times and it takes 800 spear thrusts, foot extractions and jumps, and 400 leverings and a liberal plastering of mud. But the final results are impressive. The alders grow so fast that, as my forester used to say, you have almost to jump back to avoid having your hat pushed off.

The grey alder, *Alnus incana*, a native of Scandinavia and central Europe, is an accommodating cousin to the common alder. Because of its ability too to fix nitrogen from the air it can grow well in poor soil where other trees could not survive, and it does not necessarily require wet ground. I

58

have planted hundreds on tips of industrial waste. Else-
where in Britain they have been used successfully for
planting on coal tips. The catkins are larger than the
common alder and they appear earlier – any time from the
end of February – and they are one of the first welcome
signs of spring.

A National Park authority, not being in the business of
timber production, must plant trees for amenity. It is very
satisfying for me to see some of the trees I planted years ago
now grown sturdy and large. We have planted hundreds of
standards, each in individual holes, the soil fed back
carefully to fill the spreading hair roots and the whole
trodden in tight. Usually a stake has to be planted with
them, rammed in deep with a maul. A good nursery
supplies trees with a developed root system, produced by
transplanting the seedlings and young trees several times.
Some roots such as birch and Scots pine are easily damaged
in lifting. I like to buy trees from some nursery in some
bleak high-altitude site. Then, planted in easier land, they
think it is their birthday and grow like mad from gratitude!
After planting the trees seem to stay almost without growth
for the first few years, but then to revisit them after a gap of
several years brings a delightful surprise. Some oaks with
poor roots which I once despaired of, have now grown large
and sturdy, their support stakes long redundant.

One must, of course, plant to a plan. It is a joy to be
presented with a neat coloured plan showing where the
planting should take place, and what the species should be.
Some draughtsman probably spent a long time in drawing
and colouring it. We duly arrive on site with a trailer-load of
trees ordered as specified. It is a suitable frost-free day for
planting. Unfortunately it is drizzling, but never mind.
Donald brings out the plan which immediately starts to go a
bit soggy, so we keep it on the Land Rover seat.

'Four Scots pine on top of the knoll,' he says.

The three of us pick up the pines, spades and stakes and climb over the fence and onto the knoll. First test with a spade produces the usual result. The soil appears to be six inches of topsoil above piles of rock. Back to the Land Rover for crowbars and mattocks. Start digging. One of the planting positions is obviously on solid bedrock, so Des moves the tree several feet.

'He's mucking up the plan,' I suggest.

Donald says something constructive (I think) and the stakes are driven in, the pine planted in the holes, and stamped down. That was hard work, so when we get back to the plan for the next instruction we lean back for a breather. It is always at this precise moment that someone calls out, 'Is this all you've got to do? What a great job you've got!'

'Group of eight birches, west side of knoll,' reads Donald. Off we go again. It is definitely mattock work. The roots are widespreading so the holes have to be wide as well as deep. We struggle among lumps of granite, and when we try to hammer in the stakes they refuse to go so we have to use crowbar and brute strength to bang out holes. So far so good. Back to Land Rover.

'Three rowans, east side of knoll.'

Exercise repeated with same difficulty. Back to Land Rover for 'bait'. We sit eating in the Land Rover for shelter. Some cursing as Donald has sat on the plan. Someone comes along.

'What a great job you've got.'

'Group of six oaks, south side of knoll.'

Some discussion about whether we have been supplied with correct oaks or not. The local oaks are nearly all sessile, *Quercus petraea*, which grow in upland areas. Sessile suggests 'seated' and indeed the acorns are stalkless and 'seated' on the twigs. The pedunculate oak, *Quercus robur*, is common to lowland Britain and deeper soils. The acorns are stalked and the leaves almost stalkless. We examine the dead leaves still on our specimens and we think we have been supplied with pedunculate. The plan however is just marked 'oaks', so never mind. They will take. Back into the drizzle to continue the work. The knoll is now slippery wet and we are slithering about and trying to keep upright on the steep bank. Tool handles get wet and sticky with mud. Hands are muddy and this is the stage when you need to find a handkerchief as your nose is running. Or you inadvertantly wipe your hot brow with the back of your hand. The oaks are eventually in, and back to the plan.

'Artificial mound south of knoll,' Donald says. 'Three *Prunus avium*, five rowans.'

We look at the mound and see thankfully that the dumped soil has settled. There should not be any stones in it either. Indeed the trees on top of the mound go in easily, but we are in trouble at the shallow edges. We spade through into solid stone.

I look at Donald. 'You know what's happened here?'

Donald shakes his head in disgust. 'Yes,' he says. 'They've covered the whole site with quarry waste and ballast, then dumped this earth on top. We'll need a pneumatic drill to get through here.'

We cannot just plant on top. If the roots cannot get a deep hold a strong gale will eventually take them out. So with some tension-reducing language we go for the crowbar and sledgehammer and at least break up the ballast below the planting holes. Then we plant. We do a thorough job. Three we are not happy with, we replant. It is now raining and it gets to be something of a struggle. By the time we get the last one in, the light of the winter day is beginning to go. We collect the tools and have a last drink from our flasks.

We are hot, dirty, and wet. Someone comes along.

'Finishing already?'

The plan is very soggy and I have to dry it out at home before filing it.

In sheep country every tree planting has to be accompanied by fencing. And the fence has to be good because the Lake District sheep are acrobatic. The local Herdwick breed are good rivals of mountain goats. Sheep eat practically anything green and no seedlings or young trees can possibly survive if they can reach them. We were presented with another planting plan, having acquired a new area of land, and we met the forestry expert who had travelled some sixty miles from his office to meet and advise us. There was a recommendation for underplanting with beech.

'What about fencing?' we asked. He looked round at the wood and then at us with surprise. 'Sheep frequently get over the walls around the wood,' I explained.

Then Donald and I nearly collapsed when he said, 'Well, a few sheep won't hurt. They don't like beech.'

A forestry expert he may have been. But he was totally ignorant on the matter of Lake District sheep.

Fences have to be good and they have to last. We pride ourselves on our fences. The secret is to fence in as many straight lines as possible and get really hefty strainers buried very deep. Strainers are the main posts placed at regular intervals and at every corner. John, our fencing expert, insists that the heavy timber should go in at least two and a half feet deep, three if possible. This work has to be done manually with spade and crowbar, and the ubiquitous rocks have to be hauled out by hand. You soon have broken fingernails and sore fingers. The absolute peak in frustration anger and hatred is when John comes along and looks into your deep hole and says, 'That's fine, but now

I'm afraid we'll have to move it a couple of feet up the hill.'
To make doubly sure it is strong the strainers at key points
are propped with additional stakes which are heeled onto
chunks of rock. Then the wire is hauled tight with the
straining tool and nailed.

Once the tree-planting, with fencing, is done it should
stay. But planning committees can change their mind.
Having carefully and conscientiously fenced off a hollow on
one property and planted it – a job lasting several weeks –
Donald and I were told that the committee had changed its
mind and had decided to fill in the hollow with soil
suddenly available from some nearby road-improvement
works. So we went to salvage the fence and trees. We
arrived too late. A bulldozer had ploughed down our
beautiful new (and expensive) fence and pushed it into the
hollow over our trees. Already there were tons of soil and
rock dumped on top. We salvaged all we could, but it was a
somewhat bitter experience.

In spite of all, sheep get into enclosures and, lacking
dogs, getting them out is a job that Olympic gold medallists
would find testing. If you are on your own you have to
contrive to drive the sheep down to a corner, then grab
them by their woolly coats and lift them over the fence. The
first part of the job is usually achieved after several
attempts; then you have to make a sudden grab at a sheep
which is normally ready to evade. Your woolly friend might
appear to be dozy and placid as she nibbles away at the
succulent grass, or the green tips of your new oak trees. She
is not even looking your way. But be not deceived. One
move in her direction, no matter how swift your rugby
tackle, and she is back at the other end of the enclosure,
sampling your Scots pines. Before you succeed bruises are
guaranteed as you reach a reckless condition of terrible
fury. It is said that the Vikings got themselves into a

63

suitable condition for blind savagery by taking a small portion of the fly agaric toadstool. The fungi is hallucinogenic. Perhaps a small portion should be included in all tree planters' tool kits to get up a suitable frenzy for the removal of sheep.

The Novices

Winter is the season for courses. The National Park has organised courses in fell-walking for young people for many years. The wardens are the instructors. The object is not to encourage more young people to take up fell-walking, but to help those who are already keen to learn the skills needed, particularly how to use map and compass, how to plan walks, and how to walk comfortably and safely. There is no classroom atmosphere, nor any pressure put on the students to do anything but enjoy themselves. Memories of the courses are all pleasant.

On an occasion I met a group at Nether Wasdale. There should have been seven, four girls and three boys. The three boys were there fifteen minutes before the meeting time, having walked from the bus at Gosforth. They were roughish looking, and spoke with broad Cumberland accents. One, Edward, was wearing trousers cut off below the knee and tied there with boot laces. I learned later that to pay the youth hostel fees for the course he had sold his drums. ('Nivver mind though, I'll get a better set yan day.') Three girls arrived later in a parent's car. They too were definitely Cumbrians, and they were pretending not to notice the boys. I looked at my watch. At the precise meeting time a Daimler came majestically into the square, and out stepped an immaculate young lady in anorak and trousers which looked as if they had been tailor made for her. 'Daddy' asked when she should be picked up the following day, and the car purred away back up the road. We introduced ourselves, unloaded unnecessary gear into the parked Land Rover, and set off walking. The girls chose to walk in one group, the boys in another.

It is always a good idea to start the walk off over a sticky bog. It helps students to know what they are in for. The girls dithered and screamed on sketchy stepping stones, and I had to tell the boys to mind their language. Then for the climb up loose rock to the ridge. I told everyone to keep together – that meant going at the speed of the slowest. I was glad to see that Emily, the immaculate one, was talking happily with her three new companions. But after a while all conversation ceased as lungs became strained. We stopped several times for rests, and at the third stop there were mild protests from the girls. Jenny, the eldest at sixteen, flapped her eyelashes at me and suggested that if she had known it was to be so hard the first day she might not have come. I told her that we were getting the difficult part over first, then it would all be easy. We had already gained a lot of height. One of the lads asked if we were going to be issued with oxygen masks.

Two hours after setting off we were walking up the easier incline on the summit ridge of Illgill Head above Wastwater Screes. The girls, realising that they were near their journey's objective, were chatting noisily about school. The sky was clear, there was a nice clean wind blowing, and I prepared to give them the surprise. They knew where they were but the path was well back from the edge of the ridge. I called them together. I told them to follow me and I walked to the edge. The view exploded in our faces. The Screes plunged downwards at our feet, 1600 feet into the clear blue of Wast Water. The girls stopped talking and there was a gasp. The mountains rolled away ridge after ridge to the north and east. Westwards there was the hummocky rich green country with toy settlements, farms and forests, to the sea. Out to sea was the Isle of Man.

There was a moment's silence, then Emily said, 'Oh! Wait till I tell Daddy about this!' I turned to the boys, half expecting a snigger or a comment, but they were as silent as the girls. Edward was trying to identify the distant mountain peaks from his map. After we had all tried Edward's exercise we climbed to the summit cairn, collected the inevitable irritating scattering of visitors' litter, and prepared for the descent. By the time we reached the Land Rover everyone was elated and friendships were being cemented. When the weekend was over, and I had returned them to Nether Wasdale they might have known each other all their lives. Furthermore Emily asked daddy if they could give the boys a lift. They did. It was some considerable time afterwards when all had completed the course that I heard that Emily had been stricken with polio and would certainly never fell walk again.

Over the years we have had some interesting characters on the courses. Norah was one. We knew we would have trouble with her as soon as she arrived at the assembly point. She was a well-built fifteen year old, (perhaps it is the modern school dinners?) wearing very tight jeans, and her eyes, from the dark depths of eye-shadow, were soon flitting towards the boys of the party. She quickly proved to be a disrupting element. She wanted to leave her rucksack behind. She pretended that she could not read a map and wanted everyone to help her. Her boots were hurting and the party was walking too fast. She wanted help over the stiles and the becks, and when we stopped for a rest she asked if anyone had a cigarette. By the end of the first afternoon she was holding hands with one lad, but by the evening session had transferred her attention to another. At the lecture she sat giggling at the back and protested when we brought her forward to a front seat. Once in her dormitory the female instructors had to practically sit on her to prevent her wandering, and she complained that 'only juveniles and hospital patients went to bed at ten-thirty.'

In spite of the warning that she should not come in tight jeans, on the subsequent weekends they seemed to get tighter and we wondered how she could possibly get in them. She failed the simple map-reading test on the third weekend, so she decided that she would have to come on another course. We agreed so long as she did something about her trousers. But again she turned up in tight jeans and as she had travelled a long way we had to allow her to stay. On a Sunday of atrocious weather she fixed her affections on a very large teenager; he must have stood six feet two in his fell boots. He was wearing a 'leather' motorcycle jacket and refused the offer of the loan of an anorak, even though it was threatening snow. Norah, however, accepted an anorak, and though the sleeves were so long that they hid her hands, she managed to look quite fetching. As the snow began to close in we revised our plans, kept off the higher fells, and went on to Lingmoor. The snow came down very heavily and in the poor visibility map-reading proved testing. Norah said it was far too cold and wet to read maps. Her large companion had to be bullied into producing his. He found map-reading difficult with Norah clutching at his hands. They both hung back and had to be constantly pushed on.

At lunch-time we had to crouch in the shelter of a small

crag to eat; the snow was still coming down and settling. We did not linger long as some of us were feeling cold – particularly, I noted, Norah's friend, who had discovered that the jacket he had was neither leather, nor warm, nor waterproof. We walked on in the snow which was coming down faster. Then there was the sudden freak change of weather. The snow flakes got heavier and wetter, then changed to sleet. As we began to descend to our parked vehicles at Blea Tarn we were walking in rain and the snow at our feet was transformed into slush. Luckily I was wearing nails, as I still sometimes do, but everyone else in our party was sliding about and falling. Norah managed to make one of her falls onto a trailing strand of barbed wire and complained that she was bleeding. There was a bad cut, through her jeans into her thigh. It needed a dressing. Jack, my co-instructor, and I discussed what we could do. Rolling up her jeans leg was impossible. Cutting the jeans along the seam would only make her more cold than she was already. There was only one solution: Jack bandaged her over her jeans.

We pressed on. As we descended the steep slope everyone was falling. If we had had ice axes they would have been of little use anyway as the snow covering was too shallow. At one stage I was standing against the slope catching people as they slid down towards me. To our surprise Norah was enjoying herself, screaming and laughing and grabbing at everyone. But when we stopped for a rest and looked down at our vehicles which seemed a long long way down a grey slippery slope below us we had another, unpleasant surprise. Norah's large companion was crying, and trembling. I asked him what was the matter. His answer was alarming: 'Will we ever get down there alive?' The cold had thoroughly demoralised him. Two of us stayed closely with him all the way down. Norah had deserted him in disgust, and by the time we reached Blea Tarn, had transferred her attention to another.

We drove quickly to a mountaineering club's hut to dry out and change. Norah had not got a change of trousers so Jean, one of the instructors, lent her a pair. The girls seemed to be a long time in their room. Jean at last emerged looking absolutely shattered. She poured herself a cup of tea with trembling hands.

'It took four of us half an hour to pull off her wet jeans,' she explained. 'No wonder she was walking stiff-legged on the last stretch.'

Norah asked if she could come on another course and promised not to wear tight trousers again.

Then there was Albert. Albert's parents must have been well off and they spoiled him. He arrived with brand-new gear, the most expensive anorak, alpine climbing boots, the best rucksack money could buy, new ice axe and crampons. He could also talk, and he talked a great deal about what he was going to do. In fact at times on the fell he had a terrible job standing upright at all and all his fellow students were delighted each time his endless conversation was interrupted by a fall and a struggle to get on his feet again. But he always got up and nothing seemed to hurt him physically, and no rude comment could hurt his feelings. He had to be told everything at least three times, and even then his behaviour was erratic.

Two things stick in my memory. One was when he walked through the snow into the village shop at Grasmere, wearing crampons on his boots and ruining the lino. The other was when I was leading him on a rock climb. I had spent a long time teaching him how to tie a bowline and how to belay himself, and the drill about when he should start climbing. He was quite sure he had got it right and I set off. On the first pitch he was all right. He climbed at my call when I was belayed, and when he reached me he tied himself on to the belay point correctly. But on the second pitch I had not reached the ledge where I was to tie on the second belay when I happened to look down and I saw him climbing after me.

'Stay where you are!' I called.

'Sorry,' he said, 'I thought you called to me to climb'. When he realised that we were both unsecured by a belay he became frightened.

'Look,' I called, 'you're not so bad there. Stay, and pay out the rope to me as I climb.'

I climbed on quickly and felt the rope jerk.

'Pay out you fool,' I cried. He was going to have us both off.

I reached the ledge, tied on to a spur, and called, 'Now climb!' By this time he was highly nervous and he had got the leg trembles; several times I had to pull the rope tight to help him in an awkward reach. When he reached the ledge and tied on I gave him a lecture. He was not on any account to climb in future until he had made sure that I had given him the O.K. I showed him again how to pay the rope out to me over his shoulder, how he was to hold me if I fell, and I told him not to jerk the rope. He said that he understood and was strangely and unnaturally quiet. I gave him time to rest, then set off.

But the fun was not over. I climbed up to the next belay and the rope came with me well. I could see him below me paying it out correctly and I could still just see him when I had again tied on. I pulled the slack, and called to him to climb when he was ready. My view of his lower body was obscured by the angle of the crag but I assumed that he was releasing himself from the belay point. But he was taking some time over it. I leaned out on the rope and looked down. To my horror I saw that in the process of untying the

71

belay he had untied the rope from around his waist too and he had only hand contact with the rope. The ledge he was on was not all that good. What to do? Tell him what he had done? He could fall off in the panic.

'Albert,' I called down as casually as I could, 'just pull the rope round your waist and tie a bowline.' He had it round his waist and was fumbling with the knot before he had realised what he had done. Then he panicked. He pressed himself against the crag.

'I – I – can't tie a bowline!'

'Then tie any knot!' I called. 'You've got plenty of rope. That knot will do! Now keep on tying thumb knots onto it until you've used all the rope up. Go on!'

As soon as I knew that there was a tangle of rope around his waist that Houdini would have had difficulty with, I hauled in the slack and held him tight.

'Now,' I called, 'I have you safe. Lean out from the rock and start climbing.'

I half-dragged him eventually to my position. I belayed him with my own hand and explained in simple language how he had to release the belay without untying himself. I told him on no account to do anything until I called to him and went up and out to the top of the crag, walked to a stout holly tree and tied the rope to it.

'Now Albert,' I called, 'untie the belay – the belay only! – and climb when you're ready.'

When he reached me, still pale and trembly, I told him what I thought of him and that a four-year-old child would shape better. He was quiet. But two hours later in the Youth Hostel he was boasting again and giving a purely imaginative account of his ascents of Shepherd's by three routes, and that he was looking forward to the next day on Gable. I caught his eye and he did not even blush.

It is not only young people on the courses who panic. On

72

our course for adults I had seven in my party and the average age was around forty-five. But they were all fit, and had done some walking, one or two a considerable amount. But they were new to walking in snow and ice. We were all well equipped for the conditions and had ice axes. It was not snowing, but it was a raw windy day and the wind was whipping up the deep-lying powdery snow into great stinging clouds. We were climbing to Harrison Stickle on Langdale Pikes by a path parallel to Dungeon Ghyll. Visibility in the swirling snow was occasionally down to a few yards and it was a fine test of navigation skills. We ate our lunch in the lee of an outcrop at the top of the ghyll, and the thin sand-like snow was pouring over the top of us and getting into our coffee and our sandwiches. We did not stay long and our visit to the top of Harrison Stickle was even briefer; it was merely a ritual touching of the summit cairns. The view below was patchy. We made for the path down to Stickle Tarn.

The path was completely obscured by wind-driven snow which was now coming from behind us. A great drift many feet thick had spread over the lip of the pass we were descending, forming a great wedge rather than a cornice, and what should have been a steep but easy slope was now formidable. I stood on the edge and looked down. To turn back into the teeth of the wind was an unpleasant prospect. I tested the snow with my ice axe and decided that it was firm enough to axe our way down. I got them all close together and told them that we would be descending diagonally, and I would cut the steps, at least at first. The snow was not hard and there was no need for them to cut at all. I had already showed them how to plunge their axe shafts in really deep to give themselves a good hand-hold and I had them all try it again.

'That's all you need to do,' I said. 'Follow me. We are

going down in zig-zags. Nothing to worry about. It won't avalanche.'

To embarrass me at this point my dog gave a joyful leap down the steep slope and went sliding and rolling down fearlessly for about seventy feet, taking with it a miniature avalanche. It was now climbing back for another try. I brought it to heel and told it off.

We started down. I cut the steps really deep and watched them all descend after me. They were all doing well, but the bearded bank clerk at the back, Bill, was leaning backwards and spending too much time on his bottom.

'Stand upright, Bill!' I called, spitting out snow. 'Use the steps and push in your ice axe.'

As we descended the snow seemed to get steeper in pitches, and I had to turn the route several times to avoid loose snow. But the farther down we got, the less wind. At a point where we were all strung out behind one another, about a third of the way down, I heard a strange howling noise. I could not make anything of it, my dog was still to heel. Then I noticed that the strange noise was coming right from the back, from Bill's clenched teeth. He was completely panic-stricken, and was now paddling down very slowly on his bottom with his axe held halfway down the shaft. What to do? Go back and tie a rope to him? But it was necessary for me to choose the route through firm snow, and to cut good steps. My party were all novices and I thought that the one lady member was showing signs of nervousness too. I called back and told Bill he was much safer standing upright, but his answer was to sit down and not move at all. Luckily Vic, our oldest member, waved and nodded to me and closed in on Bill.

'Come on, lad,' he said. 'Put your feet into these steps and get hold of your axe like a walking stick.'

Bill stopped howling and came gingerly on while I

74

watched. I moved to a position directly below him so that if he did slide down I would belay with my axe and stop him. But he seemed to have a bit more confidence and we moved on.

Several times as I thought we were making good progress the strange howl would go up again and we stopped for long periods as Bill, with a reassuring chat from Vic, caught up with us. These delays though, and the steep prospects below, also made the other members of the party a little apprehensive. The descent seemed to be endless and the slope got no easier. Several times there were shouts as steps crumpled, but they had all got the hang of using the whole of their axe shafts to hold themselves. At last we reached easier slopes and eventually, when I felt we were near enough to a point where the angles levelled off below, while Bill still teetered gingerly behind, I had them practice cutting steps. Then I called them in close and reminded them of the method of using the pick of the axe as a brake so that a slip could become a controlled descent. Now we would all try it. They were to do what I did. I dropped on my side and pushed off, allowing myself to pick up a turn of speed, then rolled onto my axe and plunged in the pick end and allowed it to brake me to a stop. They all tried it except Bill. In fact they climbed back up several times to have further goes. But Bill, white with apprehension, was still coming down step by step.

When Bill eventually reached the tarn at the bottom of the path I had a closer look at his boots. The heels were very worn. Even so he should have trusted his axe, I told him. As sometimes happens when a person has just come through a crisis safely, his morale swung the other way and he became ebullient and chatted gleefully away to us for the rest of the snow-free descent.

A great deal of time on courses is spent teaching would-be mountaineers to trust their equipment. The first climbs are done nervously in spite of the fact that the students know that they are secured with a sound nylon rope, and that boot soles will quite comfortably stay put on narrow footholds. Compasses rarely fail, yet students have to be convinced that they tell the truth. Ice axes have to be shown to be a useful tool with which one can trust one's life. In the event of a slip and fall on steep snow and ice it would be an automatic reflex to thrust the axe into the snow with full body weight on it. This should stop the slide. The drill then is to kick a foothold in the snow, get upright, and if necessary use the axe to cut footholds back to safety. I spend hours teaching a group of youngsters to get the hang of it – and to enjoy practising the new-found skill, yet in an emergency they can still forget.

We were walking on snow and patches of ice along a contour in Scandale using our ice axes as 'third legs' to help us over the tricky terrain. I was leading from the rear with an experienced youngster as first man, testing as he went and cutting steps when necessary. We were all enjoying ourselves when he called back, 'Take care here. There's a frozen beck covered in snow. You can step over it.' We all dutifully took care until one of the girls reached the hazard, did not step over but stood on the ice, slipped, and she was away. She picked up some speed. I called, 'Axe!' but the first thing she did was scream, and the second thing was throw her axe away. I plunged over the edge and accelerated down on my side in an attempt to overtake and stop her, but she hit a small holly tree and hung onto it. I stopped myself, told her to stay where she was, retrieved her axe, and had her cut steps back up to the path. Then I gave her a lecture, and at the first safe bit of slope we found I had her demonstrate to us that she could stop a slide if she really wanted to.

The best place to practise ice axe braking is on a steep crisp slope which levels off or, better still, rises again at the foot. Even if the students do not get it right they can then stop safely. They soon find that the sensation of sliding and stopping oneself is great fun, and climb up and slide down again like yo-yos. We can then graduate to longer slopes and harder snow. This increases speed and successful braking brings confidence. After one such exercise on the High Street range, one of the youngsters pointed out that we were merely dropping on to our backs or sides to start the descent. What happened if the walker fell down the slope head-first?

'No problem,' I said. 'If you dig the ice axe in in the same way you can pendulum into the right position and it will work just the same.'

'Show us!' several of the youngsters said.

I could not avoid it. I deliberately allowed myself to go head-first down the icy slope. I was wearing shiny water-proofs and I was surprised at the rapidity with which I accelerated. I pushed in my axe, pivoted round to the feet-first position but by this time I was travelling very fast indeed. The hard snow which looked smooth was in fact hummocky and was knocking seven bells out of my body. The pick was throwing up an impressive curtain of ice crystals way over my head and it seemed a long time before I began to slow down. When I did stop, kicked in my toes and stood up, I was considerably bruised, but I did not want the youngsters to know this and made a normal ascent to them. No one else tried the head-first technique being, I hope, convinced by my impressive demonstration. It was not until I got in the bath that evening that I could assess the extent of the damage. All in a good cause.

Every person who has spent a good deal of time in the hills is bound to have had a few frights. I had an experience

77

on one of our courses. That particular winter's day we were on the Buttermere fells and I was leading my youngsters on a descent. I was in front. The ground was frozen very hard indeed and the temperature was well below zero. The light was beginning to fade. We were crossing Buttermere Moss. Normally it is a large sphagnum bog, far too wet to cross. But this day it was frozen hard and bearing our weight; it made an ideal short-cut to the hostel. The collapse of the section I was on was very sudden. My legs went through the ice and sphagnum into bitter-cold liquid mud. And I was sinking. I could not pull myself out, as the ice could not stand the weight of my clutching hands and it was breaking up around me. I was soon in to my waist and still sinking, and I was struggling to push back to the safer surface I had walked off. But the bog was continuing to suck me down. Luckily my party consisted of some strong boys. One of them grabbed my anorak, another came up and got a hold too and the others hung on to them. There were confused shouts of 'Pull!' 'Come on, get hold!' They pulled me backwards towards safer ground, but to my alarm the lower part of my body was still sinking. I propped myself up on my elbows on the sill of the firmer ground. The mud was around my stomach. But now there were more hands holding on and heaving. There was a call to heave together. Nothing happened at first, then I was being slowly pulled out and onto my back. Eventually I slithered out and we made for sound earth where we all lay on the frost and gasped for breath. On the walk down to the hostel the mud up to my chest at the front and to my shoulders at the back began to freeze.

Some time later I was recounting my experience to a local man.

'Buttermere Moss?' he said. 'Horses have been lost in there.'

Foot and Mouth Emergency

I still remember very well that feeling of being an alien that a serviceman has on going on leave, particularly if he comes fresh from a sustained period of combat or tension. From a completely ordered, disciplined and purposeful existence he finds himself among civilians whom he soon regards as a different, aimless form of humanity, grumbling at imagined hardships, talking largely trivial gossip, and generally existing without direction or dedication. Some servicemen after a week of leave, although they might never admit it, are only too anxious to get back and away from these strange and pitiful people. I can therefore understand the distrust, incredulity and bewilderment that the hill farmer, dedicated to his work every day of the year, must often feel towards the visitors on his hills. Indeed, I am always amazed at the superhuman tolerance that the hill farmer shows to the 'non-combatants', and the hospitality he often offers is little short of miraculous.

Consider his job. He tends a large flock of animals grazing an area which might take the best part of two days to walk around – terribly rough land rising upwards to between two thousand and three thousand feet. Most of the grazing is open fell but the proper flock management depends upon a regular system of moving sheep upwards to the high grazing and downwards to the better enclosed 'intake' land, and the lower lusher 'inby' land. He has also to grow a hay crop vital for winter feeding. He has to worry about his flock through severe hill winters, first bringing in the unseasoned young stock and the older ewes ('yows') who are beginning to lack the strength to face the savage hill conditions. He has to dole out the winter hay ration and look to the mineral feeds. If snow persists he must intensify feeding and bring sheep into more sheltered areas, and often he might have to seek and dig out buried stock.

May brings lambing time and he has to be out from first light to dusk, day after day (often in foul weather), dealing with difficult births, making sure that ewes are accepting their maternal duties, and that lambs are taking feed, bringing the problem families in closer into prepared pens, and pushing the successful outwards. All births complete, he has to mark, castrate, watch for further health problems and for marauding crows and foxes. Later comes another time for mad activity with haymaking and clipping. Clipping also gives him more opportunity for closer inspection and for dipping, treating, dosing, injecting against the complaints that sheep are heir to, including flesh parasites, worms, footrot, liver fluke, dysentry, pine and scab.

Then in the autumn he has to make decisions on what sheep to sell and where, and he has to pick them out, lug them to market and get the best price he can. Then he gathers again when the first fierce signs of winter come, for it is tup time, and he has to make sure that all the eligible ewes are mated. Winter is the time for all the other routine jobs to be done: wall and fence repairs, hedging, draining. It is a back-breaking, worrying and very demanding business.

There is no answer to the layman's question, 'Why do you do it?'

It requires a great leap of imagination. 'It's a way of life' is a grossly inadequate cliché. One farmer who was asked why told me categorically and with typical irony, 'Because we're stark raving mad. Because, although our fathers, grandfathers, and mebbe back to our great great grandfathers worked themselves daft at sheep farming and nobbut-just survived, we – without the labour around that they had – we're stupid enough to believe that we can do better, and actually make money!'

To make anything of hill farming the farmer must belong to that special brand of stubborn, uncompromising, down-to-earth, thick-skinned humanity that only generations of living among the hills can breed. For he faces a constant battle against the overwhelming odds of bad weather, plague, disaster and bad luck. Add to that the fact that in our National Park visitors, huge numbers of whom come at the vital lambing time, and who have no idea of what farming is about, and worse still visitors' dogs, disturb the flocks, interfere with the grazing pattern, trespass on precious hay grass, damage walls and fences, open gates and forget to shut them, and generally tramp all over the grazing land as if they owned it. One would not blame the hill farmer if he were violently anti-social. I would be. But he is not. The Lake District hill farmer is incredibly tolerant. Oh, he can grumble! It is part of a warden's job to listen to the grumbles sympathetically and try to help, if he can, with solutions to persistent problems. The biggest grumble is that a warden is not around when it is all happening. With a 'beat' of a hundred square miles the warden cannot be everywhere.

We in fact are often around when visitors are offending. But in the long term there is more to be gained by education. And on the whole the visitors are sympathetic and eager to learn. 'Farm open days', organised to show the public the farmer's work, often receive embarrassingly large numbers of people. Indeed, if too strong an attempt was made to satisfy public demand for farm open days, farming might become impossible.

But the attraction is probably the romantic idea of hill farming. It is, after all, so picturesque. The sheep are effective lawn mowers and the hill farms are clean green from valley to hill top in the sunshine. In this delightful landscape move handsome woolly sheep and even prettier gambolling lambs, and there is this marvellous brooding figure of a man leaning on his crook with his faithful eager dogs poised for his command. If farm open days are not just entertaining 'zoo' visits and give a more realistic picture, well and good. If they do not, they might as well not be organised at all.

'What would you do,' asked the late 'Cubby' Acland, regional agent for the National Trust, in the 1960s, 'if there was an outbreak of Foot and Mouth disease in the National Park?' and he let us think about it for a while. The probable consequences were staggering. All those carefully bred 'heafed' sheep, descended from stock that had been on the fells for centuries would have to be shot and burned. If the hill farms ever recovered from such a blow, and even if the farmers were compensated massively, it would take many years for the right stocks to build up again, and in that time the landscape would change beyond recognition.

'How would we isolate the disease,' asked Cubby, 'if it hit one corner? If we isolated the infected area we would still have to keep the visitors away and prevent them from walking on the fells from suspected areas to non-infected areas. You, and every volunteer you could lay hands on, would have to stand guard, and stop the visitors from walking. There would have to be a big publicity campaign. Have we got emergency plans?'

We thought about it for a while and then decided with a shudder to think of something more pleasant. But in November 1967 Cubby's concern became reality. Britain was hit by an unprecedented epidemic of Foot and Mouth disease and large areas were devastated. It did not seem to be a threat to the Lake District at first, but as the areas spread there was the prospect of many hundreds of weekend visitors from infected areas seeking to enjoy some Lake District fell walking. Then suddenly the disease was into the fringes of the county and it was time to act.

I made hurried visits to the local offices of the Ministry of Agriculture, the National Farmers' Union, and to police headquarters, and told them of our intentions. All they did was to express appreciation and wish us luck. First the Information Service had to produce posters, and large banners were erected at the main road approaches to the National Park, asking people to keep off the fells. There were news conferences. I got in touch with Outdoors Pursuits Centres and courses were cancelled or rearranged. The Youth Hostels Association agreed to close hostels. But I had to prepare a guard of large numbers of volunteer wardens at all the approaches to the fells. There were rotas to arrange, people to find to fill gaps. Then I went to Carlisle Castle to ask for the help of the Territorial Army. The commanding officer, Lt Colonel Thompson, was extremely sympathetic. 'Tell us when and where you want a guard and you've got it.' There were offers of help too from Mountain Search and Rescue team members. Some individual farmers, recruited by the NFU also put their names to a rota. The big job was to deploy all these volunteers weekend after weekend.

The job was distasteful. Normally thousands of walkers

seek to enjoy hill walking in winter. Publicity by press, television and radio kept many day-visit walkers away from the National Park, but hundreds still came. The London headquarters of the Ministry of Agriculture did not help as they were telling telephone inquirers that it was all right for them to come to the Lake District but that 'walking might be restricted'. It is almost impossible to walk in the Lake District without crossing through farm land, and the open fell too had to be out of bounds. Only the forests were safe areas, for deer are not subject to the disease.

So the guards on the popular footpaths to the fells were asking people politely to walk only on the roads or in the forests. Ironically we had weekend after weekend of keen cold sunny weather – ideal walking conditions. Many guest-houses and hotels had cancellations, to their financial loss. It was aggravating that some holiday guest-houses with booking offices in the south of England turned no bookings down as their inquiry to the Ministry was answered only with 'there might be some restrictions on walking'. When I visited them and checked their guest lists it was clear that as many as half their holidaymakers were from heavily infected areas. They cooperated by keeping their cars in the house grounds and all walking was to be done on roads and in forest. Some of the guests, however, complained to me that if they had known about the restrictions they would not have wasted their money. I urged them to enjoy what they had got.

When I visited the manageress of one guest house, the small belligerent elderly lady, told me that she had full bookings and as far as she was concerned her guests could walk where they wanted. It was all a lot of nonsense. None of her guests came from infected farms, they were all townspeople. I told her that nevertheless they were from infected areas of the country, that the disease was highly contagious and if it came to our area it would be a major disaster.

'I think,' she complained, 'that you're one of those people that just like to make it difficult for other people. It makes you feel important.'

I swallowed this and explained that I was not asking her guests to go home, but merely to keep off farm land and the open fells. She repeated that it was all nonsense so I asked her if I could call again after dinner that evening to speak to her guests. At least she agreed to that. I returned, driving thirty miles and using up valuable organising time, to speak to her guests over coffee. I told them all something about hill farming and the seriousness of the situation. They were cooperative if at first not completely happy. But then we discussed useful walks that they could do in the area and it was surprising how many options there were. The manageress eventually walked with me to the door. She was still unrepentent, but she said, 'I'll give you this – your chat about where they could walk wasn't so bad. If you ever feel like dropping in at the same time now and then and telling the guests where to walk – a lot of them don't know where to start.'

An anonymous caller told me that a certain climbing club with premises in the area were having a big meet at the weekend and they intended climbing on certain crags regardless of the emergency. I drove round on the Saturday morning to see them. If they wanted a fight, I thought, right was on my side. Some of them had had a very boozy night, were just out of bed and not in a good mood. However they all listened to what I had to say, but I kept my eye on one man who was banging breakfast pots around and was obviously building up some hostility. It exploded.

'Look. Between the road and the crag what is there? Just ferns and rock. No grass. No sheep. Me and my mates are climbing and you nor anyone else will stop us. You can't.'

I told him that it was quite correct that I hadn't the power to stop him. But it was intake land and it had grass and sheep and he certainly had no right of access to the crag. He was there normally by courtesy of the landowner and the tenant farmer. Did he really want a confrontation with the farmer? Enjoyment of facilities by the club depended upon maintaining happy relationships. And did he really want it widely known that all the climbing clubs were willing to cooperate except this one? He was still showing symptoms of aggression so I told him that later that day I was meeting a television crew for an interview. If he liked I would persuade them round and he could argue his case for access to the crag. The interviewer would jump at the chance to come. They love controversy. He might interview a local farmer too. It might go out nation-wide. He quietened down and did not accept the offer. The club secretary was smiling and said, 'Don't worry. We'll cooperate. It won't be for ever anyway.' He walked with me down the drive to the road.

'What we'll do this weekend,' he said, 'is a monumental spring-clean of the hut that we've been threatening to do for years. And we have some paint and brushes. Don't worry about Frank, he'll calm down. He's a great bloke really. We'll harness his energy. We'll have him organise a foot race to the pub at lunch time.'

When we got to the landrover he was smiling, and looking at me sideways.

'That bit about the TV crew. Bloody blackmail, wasn't it?'

'I reckon,' I admitted. But I *was* being interviewed and I meant what I said.

Evenings were a constant succession of telephone calls. Offers of help, volunteers for instructions, and inquiries, mainly from would-be visitors who could not believe what they had heard or seen in press, radio and television. Climbing and rambling clubs rang, hoteliers, Study and Outdoor Pursuits centres. A few calls were abusive. It saddened me in the middle of this when I had a call from a farmer, a personal friend, one evening – not to congratulate us for the efforts being made, but to complain bitterly that his area was being neglected. We had excellent support from the media, but an outrageous report in one paper stated that some of the guards I was using came from infected areas. As I had taken great pains to vet every offer of help, refusing help from our own voluntary wardens if they were anywhere near an infected area, this caused me some bitterness. The reporter assured me that his source of information was normally highly reliable, but agreed to have the allegation retracted.

The 'guards' were on duty for nine weekends until the crisis had diminished. There were few incidents of unpleasantness. At Haweswater one walker who refused to be deterred complained that he was threatened. I was told the story later. He was a confronted by a keen young man of the Territorial Army who said nothing when the man offered to walk on but loaded cartridges into his rifle. The man said, 'You wouldn't have me believe that you would use that thing?'

'I don't know,' replied the young man. 'I'm just a farmer's lad and new to this game. I've been told I have to obey orders. Orders are to stop anyone going up this path. Sergeant's not about so I can't ask him. I suppose I'll just aim for your legs or something like that.'

The man decided to turn back.

On some of the early days of the operation we were meeting and advising some two thousand and more would-be fell walkers. The numbers declined dramatically as time went on, but rose again during the Christmas holiday period. The suggestion to my authority that we withdraw the restrictions was my own. No one at the Ministry would take the responsibility of offering advice on this point. Understandably towards the end there were fewer volunteers for what was a boring job. The work was very wearing, but what was amazingly gratifying was the enormous amount of support we got from the hill walkers and climbers. Many of their 'huts' were closed down. Others only opened for meetings, Christmas parties, and repair parties. The climbing crags, the popular hills, were deserted. The valley heads were incredibly quiet. Very few were tempted onto the fell by the fine weather. Only towards the end were there signs of impatience. Gratitude is owed too to the Youth Hostels Association, and the hotel and guest-house owners who made financial sacrifices.

What would have been pleasant was a final whisper of appreciation of all the support from some official quarter. It did not come. From the farmers themselves we expected nothing. I feel that in a national park they had a right to receive our help and they got it. But they got something else too. When a farmer is under great pressure it is understandable if he views the activities of relaxed and carefree visitors with distrust and bewilderment. But the public response to the crisis proved irrefutably that there was a great reserve of sympathy and support.

Tilberthwaite Ghyll

October usually has some reasonably dry weather, but in the Lake District one has to be prepared for the unexpected. I arranged to meet Eric, a voluntary warden who was an engineer, at Tilberthwaite to investigate the route of a path in the centre of a deep ravine. The path existed on the official map but was thought to be the figment of some draughtsman's imagination. We knew that the path from the top of the ravine was fairly easy to follow; in Victorian times it had been a popular tourist attraction and there were remnants of the bridges that had been put in. But having descended by the ghyll to a point near a waterfall, one was faced with a drop below and wet high walls of rock on either side. The only feasible way out was back up the path one had just followed. The object of the inspection was to see if a new section of path could be engineered from the bottom of the ravine.

The ravine is beautiful. Water pours down its centre and is fed by scores of springs trickling down the sides. The hollow rings with the sound of water, rushing, falling, splashing, dripping. Being too steep for grazing, the sides are heavily wooded with ash and oak and larch, self-seeded.

The brown soil on the banks are mineral rich and lush with green plants, ferns, mosses, and liverworts. Halfway down the ravine is the waterfall, gushing between the narrows of steep crag walls and projected outwards to pound into a deep pool. After heavy rain it roars and sprays with some passion and that is the time to see it, with ferns, branches, twigs bright with droplets, and the white water pounding step by step down the dizzy depths.

On the day of our meeting it rained relentlessly until the water poured in cascades down every fell, and the roads were awash in places. But we had arranged to meet and meet we did. Festooned in waterproofs, we looked at the ravine, roaring and shaking with the pressure of falling torrents. Every feeder, every spring, was cascading water. There was no hope of seeing anything in the ravine except water and we laughed about it and discussed another date. We were then suddenly aware that the female occupant of a parked car was bearing down on us in a state of agitation.

'Please can you look for my husband?' she called. 'He went to take a photograph of the waterfall and hasn't come back.'

'How long has he been gone?' I asked.

'Two hours,' she said.

I tried not to show concern. The waterfall was a mere ten minutes away.

'He must have fallen in,' she cried, and burst into tears.

I looked at Eric. 'You go up the left bank,' I suggested, 'and have a good look. I'll go up the right bank in a moment and if we don't see him we'll meet at the top on your side of the ravine.'

I led the lady to the nearby group of cottages. One of the cottagers sold teas and I left the lady with them and asked them to take care of her. I then wrote a note and left it in the car to tell the man, in case he returned in our absence, where he could find his wife. Then I walked up the right-hand side of the ravine.

The water was raging high and very fast. If the man had indeed slipped in, he would by now have been swept away, probably down into the river but he would almost certainly have been killed first in the fall. Our only hope was that he had survived a fall and was clinging to a bank, or, overcome by panic, was cragfast on some ledge. To fall in when taking a photograph would be the easiest thing in the world. Watch rushing water for only a short time, particularly through a camera viewfinder, and vertigo is almost certain. So I was apprehensive.

I clambered along the bank, peering into the torrent until I reached the falls. I looked down the thundering white water into the swirling pool at its base and could see nothing. Eric on the other side was shouting and waving. I spread out my hands to indicate that I could not hope to hear what he was saying above the din of falling water, and he pointed upwards to show that he had searched on his side at this point and was moving up. This was the big waterfall; but there were others above and a keen photographer would no doubt walk on for more shots. I had a look round at the wet banks to see if there were any signs of footprints of slip marks, but no prints could last in the downpour for long. I walked on up a very exposed and treacherous path under larch trees and continued on as close to the ravine as I dared. Below me the trees were so thick that if anyone had fallen here he would lodge in the branches. I looked for anything – articles of clothing, broken branches, any sign of landslips. The sound of water had almost made me deaf. Water was oozing out of my boots. Water had found the gap between hood and neck in my waterproof and was creeping into shirt and sweater. And still it rained. The cloud had thickened even more and the light was getting worse. I continued the search upwards, hanging onto branches and roots where necessary; there was no sign of man or clues.

Some fifteen minutes later I was at the top of the ravine. I looked across through the veils of drifting rain and spray but could see no sign of Eric. Well, I did say I would go across to meet him. However, to say it was one thing, to do it was another. Normally it is possible to top the head of the ravine by jumping the deep but narrow ghyll pouring into it. But instead of one waterflow there were a dozen pouring into the ravine from a large fan-shaped area of falling water above. I went upwards to the first stream of this wide fan, but it was impossible to cross; so I ascended the fell until I found a place where it was sufficiently narrow. But I did this only to find myself facing another stream and the same problem, then another and another as I climbed farther up the fell. It took me half an hour, and sometimes I was up to my knees in fast-flowing water, or gripped tight by black mud, or floundering through deep wet blankets of sphagnum moss, ballooning under their weight of water. Once or twice I was frightened. But at last I made it and I saw Eric waving to me from a knoll, the only island among the water.

'Any sign?' I called as I eventually reached him.

'No, let's go back. With luck he may have made it before us.'

We scrambled down the rock steps and the steep grass; all of it was flowing with water. The whole surface of the world was flowing with water and still it rained. We reached the road awash with water; the bridge was inundated. The car was still there. The note was still in place on the seat.

'I'm afraid it's a matter for a rescue call-out,' I said. 'You stay here with the car. I'll phone, then I'll collect the lady and take her into the police station. I'll wait there for the team to assemble and come back with them.'

I waded across to the cottage to find to my annoyance that the storm had put the phone out of action. The poor woman was now in a state of shocked panic in spite of the kindness of the cottagers. I comforted her by suggesting that the man might have got lost and made his appearance at the police station. I suggested that she go there with me. She climbed into the Land Rover and we drove down to the valley.

A mile on, limping along the road, was a very wet gentleman looking decidedly the worse for wear.

'Is that him?'

The lady screamed, 'Yes!'

I jumped out when we reached him. His wife was struggling with the door handle and she could not follow me for a moment.

'I got fast between two streams,' he said wearily. 'I had to climb high, then I got lost when I tried to get back.'

But his wife, in a highly emotional state from relief and/or severe shock, was then on to him, thumping his chest with both her fists.

'You stupid – stupid man! Where have you been you stupid, stupid idiot!'

She continued in similar vein as I pushed them into the Land Rover. On the drive back she rose to a crescendo of hysterical abuse. I left them at their car and gave the man some Kendal mintcake to suck. Eric stood with me in the still heavy rain listening with fascination to the female vocal cannonade. Then he turned to me, rain pouring from his hood.

'Reckon we'll have to fix another date to look at the ravine.'

'I reckon so,' I answered. But we never did.

Felling

'Let's have no romantic ideas about working in the forest. A forest is about timber production. You should remember that the forest is a factory floor.'

I burned when I heard this. The speaker was a young man who was instructing us in 'safety at work' and the implications of the new Health and Safety at Work Act, particularly in the use of chainsaws. Some of the 'students' had been forest workers before the instructor was born and to hear this nonsense from someone still wet behind the ears was ridiculous.

And the forest a factory floor? God help us, no. Neither is a farm, a smallholding or a garden. They are living, breathing communities and their successful cultivation and cropping depends upon a close working relationship with nature. Factory forestry and factory farming are abominations. They are dedicated to short-term gain and long-term devastation. When they do not offend the eye they are immensely boring. For a moment I was so angry with the young man I felt like starting my chainsaw and giving him a short back-and-sides haircut.

The factory forest is staying with us. Alas, there are good

arguments for planting the large blocks of straight-lined conifers in the modern forest. It is transforming otherwise useless land to commercial productivity. It is conserving and improving poor soil and providing new habitats for wild life. In the long term it provides so-called recreational facilities for the public, with forest walks, nature trails, picnic sites, camping areas. Fine. But the much more colourful, interesting, soil-enriching broadleafed wood-lands with their extensive varieties of natural habitats are being superseded. Our native trees that have been with us since the ice ages are falling before the coniferous invaders from North and Western America, Scandinavia, the Alps and the Pyrenees and Japan. There is hardly any visible spring or autumn in our factory forests of spruce, in contrast with our broadleaf woodlands – there is only a perpetual green. And we are destroying our heritage of woodlands, clear felling them, even killing them with defoliant sprays to replace them with conifers for a quick return.

'Oaks don't grow well in this soil anyway,' explained the agent as we watched one huge wood falling to the saws.

'But people have lived on them hereabouts for a few thousand years,' I suggested.

'Coppicing though,' he said. 'There's no return on coppicing today and there aren't the men to do it.' The woods we were watching being felled had many other uses. The report of the King's Commissioner of 1537 on the woods of Furness in the Lake District, owned by Furness Abbey until the Dissolution, records that in addition to timber '... there ys another yerely profytte commyng and growing of the said Woodes, called Grenehew, Bastyng, Blecking, Byndyng, making of Sadeltrees, Cartwheles, Cupes, Disshes, and many other thynges wrought by Cowpers and Turners, with making of Coles, and panage of

95

Hogges, according as hath always ben accustomed to be made in the said woodes...'

The woods then not only provided building material, furniture and fuel, but the cups and dishes, bark for the tanning of leather and the dyeing and bleaching of wool, oak strips for basket making, staves for barrels, 'bast' for making cordage and mats, 'panage' too – ground fodder for pigs, charcoal for iron smelting and later for making gunpowder. Stone houses were framed with wood.

The natural hardwoods of Britain were thus the foundations of prosperity. They produced the rich soil on which agriculture was based. The ships which made trading possible were built from them. Forests were regarded as so valuable that several acts of parliament were made for their protection. Forests were carefully maintained for many centuries – 'coppiced', felled in rotation, and the new shoots from the 'stools', the stumps, allowed to regrow into substantial new trunks for future cutting.

But they are going. Hardwoods do not grow fast enough. They often occupy good agricultural land – land they have made good – but they must be cut down in the interests of food production. Conifers are more profitable. It is to the advantage of land owners to plant conifers. The National Trust do their best to preserve and plant hardwoods at some considerable cost, and some of the old woods are Nature Reserves.

The Forestry Commission have statistics to prove that the majority of visitors to the forests like conifers. Well, I like conifers. I like any trees. Give me a thousand acres of thick spruce forest in some bleak place where no trees grew before and I will cheerfully walk in and get lost in it. But it is unutterably sad to see oak, yew, ash, elm, birch, hazel, even the alien but long-accepted beech and sycamore, fall to the saw to make way for the conifer factory forest.

I have conflicting feelings about the chainsaw which has made factory forestry possible. The chainsaw has done for the forester what the wellington boot did for the farmer. It has made life much easier. The modern chainsaw is a far cry from the Neolithic stone axe. It was not all that long ago when all forestry was done by an axe not much different in shape from the Scafell's factory axe. I was axe trained. My felling axe lived under my bed protected from those who might dare to borrow it. Now axes are hardly used. Tree felling was a relatively quiet, hard-slogging, contemplative operation. It was also skilled precision work. The axe became part of you, a sort of controlled extension of yourself. But start up a chainsaw, and from its first roar of life you realise that you have a tiger by the tail. It snarls, bares its teeth, and strains to have a go at your trousers or your boots, and in sheer self-defence you have to plunge it into wood, which it bites into savagely like some mad starving animal.

In felling, the 'laying in' or the cutting of the 'gob', the first deep bite out of the side of the tree on which it must fall – was cut carefully and precisely by the axe. The chainsaw has no time for such care. The gob is open in a matter of minutes, and the saw, overcome by bad-tempered rage, strains and screams to have a go at the other side. What matter if the tree does not fall precisely where you wanted it? It is not so far out, and anyway you can move quickly up the tree to 'sned' away any caught branches in seconds. And the noise? Ear muffs are worn defensively – with a safety helmet which is really needed to protect you from the trees falling in all directions from the other half-mad chainsaw users on the 'factory floor' around you. And, oh brother! when there is a chainsaw accident it is really spectacular! Imagine, if gunpowder had not been invented, what great bloody battles could be fought by

chainsaws! I swear too that this fiendish instrument culti-
vates the aggressive instincts in its operator just as a
big-engined, fast sports car transforms a mild and ordinary
motorist into a power-mad maniac. We have a fitting for
one of our chainsaws – a tungsten-carbide cutting wheel
which can cut through steel. In a matter of minutes almost,
an old abandoned eyesore of a car can be cut into sections
like a loaf of bread. And I have this dream of walking
calmly into some particular office paradise, the Department
of Arrogant Prevarication, starting the machine up and
reducing desks, chairs, and filling cabinets into small
parcels.

But, to be fair, it used to be a very tough job indeed to
reduce an oak trunk to fireplace lengths for fuel. Now I can
slice up a trunk in minutes, just dropping my chainsaw onto
it and letting its own weight and ferocity do the work. So I
bless it as well as curse it, as the infantryman once did his
gun. It is a millstone and a source of worry and it is a
life-saver. Felling and 'snedding' (cleaning off the branches) in a conifer forest with a chainsaw is a boring
factory-floor job. But praise be the National Park Authority's woodlands are hardwoods mainly and every thinning
or felling job offers a variety of problems and solutions.
None so enjoyable perhaps as the felling on our Windermere islands. The felling is necessary to open up some of
the tree canopy to allow light in for seedlings to grow, and
to plant more trees. The aim of good woodland management is to have a 'spread' of age groups in the trees so that
there is everything from young saplings to full mature trees.
This means that the wood is perpetuated and will not
suddenly die from old age.

We hired a workboat and contracted two men and a boy
for the felling jobs and by early light of the November
mornings we were chugging across to the islands in the

heavy low-gunwaled craft, with out bait and tea flasks in our haversacks, and the chainsaws wrapped in sacks. Most of the mornings were cold, nose-and-finger-biting, frosty ones, with the lake cloaked in white mist. We would set off in the rough direction of the islands without having them in sight, and before we reached them we would see their tree crowns nebulously hovering above the mist. It would be some time before we saw the banks. Sometimes the boat grounded before we reached them. On one day it was so foggy we had to have a debate as to whether we were on Lilies of the Valley island number one, or number two. It turned out that we were on neither but had reached Tommy Holme (Thompson's Holme). Sometimes the dawn would rise scarlet and the whole of the lake looked like rippling fire. Sometimes it would be purple – so purple that if I had taken a colour photograph one would suspect afterwards that I had a faulty film. Sometimes the water would be still and calm like plate glass, with perfect reflections of the tree-girt hills, and we would watch the bow wave fan out behind to set them a-tremble, jerking up the idle mallard. The water birds were always our companions and I would watch for my favourite friends the cormorants, mysteriously reptilian as they dived and reappeared, and swam like surfaced submarines with most of their body underwater.

The disembarkation was accomplished either by a leap from the high bow if we were wearing boots, or a splash through the shallows in wellies, and we were alone on the island which in the summer might be invaded by picnic parties. The trees were close-packed and we started on the perimeter ones with their great crooked heads which grew outwards for the light and hung over the water. There was the difficulty. They could only fall one way, into the lake, and to lop and top them, and log them to portable lengths meant winching them back onto the island after doing some

99

perilous de-branching from precarious perches, or from the workboat.

Cutting the gob, on the side it was to fall, was also a hazardous business. It usually meant standing in the water and if the water was deep waist-length waders were needed. It was, we found, difficult to assess precisely the depth of the clear water as we peered into it as the stones on the bottom were magnified. It was prudent to test with a pole, for a miscalculation meant that the water came over the wader tops with freezing and breathtaking results. We had also to start the chainsaws before stepping into the water and hold them above the surface, which was tiring. So having cut the gob, with the mass of saw dust floating on the water and reminding me vaguely of semolina pudding, it was with some relief that the engine was switched off and it was possible to struggle back to land.

It was then necessary to make the back cut, and because the weight of the tree leaned away at an acute angle, it was as well to be ready for a sudden collapse. The trees fell with a crack and a splash, spreading great ripples outwards, and the next job was to decide the sequence of cuts to reduce the tree to movable lumps. No use rushing it. A mistake might mean the embarrassment of having your saw jammed immovably, a victim of its own greed, in the crushing fibres of the broken trunk. With luck you could extricate it with a wedge and hammer (to the sarcastic comments of your colleagues) or you might have to suffer the humiliation of asking someone to cut your saw free.

No, it was no easy task, but interesting. No factory floor boredom about it. The job was slow too because every piece of timber had to be boated or floated ashore. There was no room on the islands to burn the toppings and a fire could damage roots and ground flora. The large trunks were saleable but some of the lengths were so green and heavy that they would not float. Against this eventuality Vince had the presence of mind to bring a large number of inflated old inner tubes with ropes for binding and towing. But this took time. There were four islands to deal with and we hoped to finish the job in three weeks, but that meant working six-day weeks and using volunteers to help us move the wood.

I remember that the largest oak I felled there was leaning out over the lake. The gob had to be cut from the lake and the water was thigh deep. I managed it without getting the saw wet and struggled back to shore. I could hear Vince and Norman, his mate, working further down the island so I was on my own and nobody in the way. The back cut was easy as I only had to drop the saw onto the leaning trunk and let the saw cut with its own weight. It gradually growled its way through from one side and I started at the other, to cover the full width of the trunk. Long before I reckoned that I had reached the point when the support was undermined and the remaining fibres would act as a hinge for the fall, there was a loud bang which I heard above the chainsaw's engine, and I felt as if I was losing my balance and falling. What was actually happening was that I had eyes fixed on the trunk and it was the trunk that was moving not me. I had forgotten to reckon the tree being hollow and rotten at the centre, which it was. I switched off the saw, whipped it out and cleared to one side. There was one splash, then a cannonade as tree branches hit the lake bed and shattered from the trunk, and then another great splash and a water spout as the massive trunk hit the lake, sank, and then very slowly raised itself. There were no other chainsaws going at that time and I heard a cry, a burst of expletives, and a roar of laughter. Norman had been standing in waders in deep water farther along the island when he was hit by the tidal wave from my tree and inundated. Vince and the boy were enjoying their colleague's misfortune.

'Sorry Norman!' I called.

'So you – ought to be!' he shouted. 'Don't worry. I'll get the lot of you!'

The next stage was tricky and required Vince's expertise. We had to hand-winch my tree trunk in; this meant taking the boat out and fastening a wire sling far along the trunk. A hook and steel hawser was fastened to this and taken back to the winch which had been anchored by another sling, padded with sacks, to a firm standing tree. All we had to do then was together work the large lever to and fro and a ratchet wheel hauled in the cable. This was not simple and we had to change the position of the sling on the trunk several times before we got it inshore. Even so a substantial part of the tree was still in water and had to be lightened.

Before I waded in I had a look around to see what stage other felling operations were at. I did not want to be caught out by someone else's tidal waves and I did not like the old-fashioned look that Norman gave me. I started the saw and took the plunge. The work was harder. I was now using the saw held high at chest level and above, and it was no light weight. It was also dangerous at this angle and I made a conscious note to flick off the switch if I lost control and the saw fell towards me. I had to stop at intervals, carry the saw to shore, and then wade back in to pull in branches I had cut. This took about an hour in all and the branches farther out were left to last. They could all be reached by wading in to near stomach depth I hoped, but before making the cuts I rested and surveyed the scene. The view was clear to the next island and the shore. The sun was shining and the frost had melted on the lake-side meadows; they shone a delicious green. Green grass in November, and on the wooded heights above the fires of autumn still glowed. The

102

oaks were warm brown, the larches platinum, and a line of silver marked the twisting route of a falling beck. There was not a sign of anyone on the shore, and the only sight of living creatures were two distant mute swans.

I eventually summoned the courage to wade out again, decided against going out too far beyond the trunk and leaned against it to cut. I was not going to risk losing my balance and falling into deep water. I had finished one cut and stopped the engine when I heard the outboard motor. I knew what it was. Vince had towed a small dinghy behind the workboat and it was fitted with an outboard. It was bearing fast in my direction with Norman at the controls and the boy with him. Both were grinning and I instantly knew their intentions. The boat was overpowered and produced a tidy bow wave. I struggled with the heavy saw to get around the trunk and to shore as fast as I could. But it was impossible to move fast in the deep water with heavy waders. I did not make it. The wave hit me and I felt freezing water pouring down my legs. I shouted some words of acknowledgement which were lost in the outboard's noise. The two were in fact shore-bound carrying a can of sump oil and some old tyres to start a fire to burn the toppings.

After emptying the waders, wringing out stockings and putting them on again, the next job was to cut away a length of trunk which was leaning over the water. It looked like the great neck and head of some primeval saurian. I felled the neck as if it was a standing tree, cutting a gob on its lower side, resting, refuelling, and then returning to make the back cut. I reckoned that if I was quick enough, when it started to fall I could struggle back to shore before it splashed down. I did not quite make it, but then I was already wet. I called to Vince that we could try winching again.

103

Not long afterwards we were sat in the workboat, all a bit wet but happy eating our 'bait' in the sunshine. Marvellous how the simplest meal tastes like a feast in the open air after strenuous work. A lump of strong cheese, a piece of raw onion, and some wholemeal crusty bread. Or a large piece of cheese and an apple – preferably a cox's. Or a thick ham sandwich with cress and cucumber. Or a spicy pasty eaten with a crunchy celery heart (they grow the best in Lancashire). Or a roast-beef sandwich with a red pepper. Or the height of decadent indulgence – a piece of Cumberland pork pie with a boiled egg in the centre. Or – if you fancy something sweet – Cumberland rum-butter on fresh wholemeal bread with raisins. Then lie back to watch the clouds chasing each other in a blue sky and to listen to the water lapping against the boat.

Not for long though. Not when days are short and it might be too wet to work on the morrow – and the fire on the shore might be starving. Next job was to load the boat with as much of the portable wood as it would carry, heavy stuff in the bottom and the lighter branches thrown on the top. This meant walking and carrying, with chainsaw bursts to make the occasional cut. At last, when the boat was loaded high and the trunks lashed astern, the trip to shore as near the bonfire as we could get. The branches thrown down by the fire, or directly onto it, the heavy stuff and the saleable lengths stacked neatly against a tree for collection.

Keeping a fire going is an art. It has to be sufficiently hot to burn the green wood which would not burn on a normal fire. Then the fire burns more quickly in the centre, and if the outer wood is not thrown inside the fire dies. When wood burns with a lot of moisture it is white hot and fierce. So much so that if you throw on some litter-lout's abandoned bottle it melts. Birch twigs explode with violent heat.

104

Green logs hiss like steam-engine valves as all their sap is thrust out under heat pressure. Any leaves still on branches rattle like fire-crackers and their red ashes spin rapidly upwards in the hot air currents.

On one of these days we were on the islands I nearly came to a watery end. A shout came from the shore. A party of Venture Scouts were there. They had offered their services in helping to clear the wood; their reward for doing it was the use of the unsalable stuff for fires at a nearby jamboree site. Vince suggested that I took the small dinghy and bring three of the scouts back to help us load, telling the rest to keep the fire going and to drag dumped wood from the shoreline.

'Take care,' said Vince. 'The throttle cable to the outboard is short and if you turn the tiller too sharply the throttle opens up.'

The boat was overpowered and I should sit as far forward as I could. I got in and the engine started first pull, which took me by surprise. The bows rose out of the water and I could not see where I was going. I had an idea that I was heading for a reef so I turned the tiller and craned my neck. The unforgettable happened. The throttle cable tugged wide open and the boat sprang forward. I was flung backwards off the seat, falling against the stern so that I could not straighten the tiller which was jammed by my left ear. I did not know where the throttle control was and I felt powerless to grope for it. The boat banked right over and went into a full-bore tight circle. I made frantic efforts to get up but centrifugal force plus my tightly jammed position were too much. Two things, I thought, could happen. The boat could turn turtle. I felt it surely would as the water was boiling round the gunwale. Or I could hit rocks. Either way I could get very wet or severely injured, and as I was wearing waders and no life-jacket, possibly severely drowned. After all, I thought, was this the ridiculous way I was to meet my end? However, after what seemed a very long superhuman struggle, I extricated myself sufficiently to straighten the tiller. As I heaved into an upright position and groped for the throttle control I was able to see the shore of the island roaring past like a green blur with three astonished people apparently staring at me with open mouths. I waved at them as I steered the projectile towards the shore and eased back the throttle. I never knew what they thought of my escapade. Strangely no one raised the subject on my return with the three scouts. Perhaps they thought I was putting the boat through its paces to see what it could do. Perhaps they thought that they had been about to see an expensive boat and outboard wiped out and that was too painful a prospect to recall.

Actually the fun was not over. We were able to load faster with the help of the scouts. Inevitably we overloaded the workboat with the result that it settled low and we could not get it in close to shore until we had off-loaded some of the timber. So the first part of the load had to be thrown ashore. Some of the branches were two-man loads and it was a matter of 'On the count of three...' However in a temporary lull in unloading only one of the older scouts on the boat was working. He had picked up an L-shaped piece and the base of the L was behind his back. We all watched as he swung the wood, 'One, two –.' I suppose we all drew breath to warn him, but too late. On his 'three' the back of the branch hit him square on his bottom and he disappeared. There was a splash and we all scrambled to the side. He came up from total immersion blowing water and held out his hand frantically. Someone grabbed it and we heaved him aboard where he gasped and floundered like a landed pike. He was very cold and we rushed him ashore to the fire, stripped off his outer gear and toasted him while it

106

steamed reasonably dry.

I think it was the same day that Vince dived in the lake to avoid being hit by a falling tree. I suppose this sort of thing would not have happened on a well regulated 'factory floor' of spruce forest. No. There would not be a single leaning tree, or an L-shaped piece of wood. Maybe factory floors are somewhat safer. But how boring!

Winter Work Party

It has snowed several inches in the night and as it is Sunday morning the roads are empty. I drive my lonely way over the hill, through the tunnel of spruce trees now bright green in contrast to their white mantles, and the lake is below me, still, unrippled, with a haze of white fog on its surface. The only sign of life in the village is the smoke rising straight from the chimneys and a few dogs on their morning rounds. I park beyond the village, pick up axe, bowsaw and rucksack, and walk down through the woods.

Not only every branch, but every twig and every fragile twiglet bears its burden of snow. As I brush through snow falls softly about my shoulders and is cold on my face. Even the lichens and the mosses on trunks bear snow. Every brown bracken frond is bowed under its weight of snow and springs back as it is disencumbered by my passage. Light saplings, lithe and supple with youth, have suddenly grown old in the night and crouch like hunchbacks over the path. I can almost hear them sigh as I shake the weight off them, and they stretch very slowly back like rheumatical worshippers rising from their knees. The browns and greens still visible in the winter woods seem almost to be glowing with an inner light. The lichens and the mosses on the low wall in the glade are particularly beautiful, and in all this waiting stillness of nature, when the whole of life seems sleeping, I look for, and find, the tiny grey fingers of *Cladonia* lichen with their bright red tips like sealing-wax, not flowers but apothecia, winter-defying store-houses of spores. Needing further proof that spring is promised I soon find an impudent (or imprudent?) honeysuckle in new bud.

As I descend the old footpath the wood becomes thicker and it seems to me that the old grey-lichened oaks are uncharacteristically gay in their snow, and stand like stern Quakers, half-ashamed at showing their new mantles. I step aside, sweep the snow off a fallen birch log with my glove, and sit down to listen to the silence. Nothing stirs. The brooding wood, the whole world, holds breath. I welcome silence. It comes to me like a balm to heal the bruises and blisters caused by the blows and abrasions of sound. I sink deeply into it, absorb it like a winter-weary bather in the sun. As I feel it restoring me I look again at the wood around me and it seems an even more special place, as if it has been hallowed by silence. I hold still and let the silence close over me so that I reach greater depths. I can hear my own pulse and the air moving in my lungs, and I feel as if I am part of all around me. For trees, plants, birds, insects are still not waiting, but poised between ebb and flow, and, as all depend on each, sharing in a mystical communion.

When I lived in the city I could only bear it so long as I could occasionally find a silent place. Silence became all the more precious. I needed to purge away the noise, to cauterize the wounds.

Most of us are afraid of silence. Silence puts us on our own, face to face with our own thoughts but also perhaps our fears. The radio is one of our ablest defences and no one who fears the threat of silence should be without a portable.

I occasionally meet radios on the fells, but they are not as common as they were when they were still a novelty. Anyone using one now in a remote place is often met with hostility by those he encounters.

'We even heard a transistor set on top of Blencathra,' grumbled a very large Yorkshireman to me one day. 'I mean, on a remote spot like that! It was the end. So I said to this fellow who had it, "It's a free country and all that, but I must warn you that me and my mate are very clumsy and we've been known to stand on radio sets – by accident." '

The offender apparently took the hint.

I leave my birchlog perch and continue to descend, footsteps silenced by the thick carpet of snow on an underlay of leaf mould. Soon I find tracks. A fox, treading delicately with footsteps neatly in line, has gone before me. I can even see the smudges left by his brush. Farther on he has turned, dug under the snow by the root of a fallen birch, then he has jumped onto the trunk and walked along it into the silent wood. There is no other sign of life except a single feather on the snow, soft, delicate, and curled, perhaps only just preened from a tawny owl as he settled himself sleepily in some nearby hollow tree. Shortly a silent movement from a bird above sends down a miniature snow fall, flakes linking hands as they descend. Then again the fox tracks in front appearing from heaven knows where. Here he has dug deep into the bank on the trail of some vole, and below he has broken into a run (did he sense my approach?) and turned off into the swamp. Now the oaks are fewer and there are coppiced alders, six or seven trunks growing from one stump; they are very tall and slender, well past the time that they should be cut again. The trunks show brown and pink, the upper sides of their leaning forms ridged with snow. Here I stop again because I have spotted a fine straight stick in a clump of hazel. It has grown vertically from a stout horizontal member and there is a handle already made. I unhook the saw from my shoulder and cut it clear, trimming it with the axe. The sound I have made has broken the spell.

The silence has melted as surely as the snow will when the sun rises higher. I have only now to move a few yards and there is the sound of softly running water for the frost has not penetrated deep enough into the sphagnum of the swamp. Well, it is very pleasant, like the soft sound of elfin conversation. But under the snow on the paths are loose rocks, and the footsteps now crunch and grind. Soon I glimpse the lake between the trees and I am standing on the shore. The water is quite still and is covered in mist. When the lake awakes from its sleep, and lifts and falls as it is stirred by the morning air, the mist will move and the ice which borders the lake edge will break up. But now it all lies still and waits.

But to work. I drop rucksack and tools on the beach by a pile of cut branches, and walk among a grove of birches, breaking off dead twiglets and shaking off their snow. This occupies me for some twenty minutes. Having put down my burden of twiglets I forage again and pull off larger dead twigs and small branches. I then choose an area of stony beach nearby and kindle my fire. Soon the work party will arrive to cut back the encroaching shrubs and branches from the lakeshore path. As I work I am suddenly aware that the light has intensified and I look over my shoulder at the lake and find that the mist has mysteriously melted. The remnants of it smoke slowly upwards like strands of hair, and hang in the trees on the far shore where John Ruskin once lived. Then there is a sigh. The day has lain abed too long and is stirring. Snow falls from the high branches of the trees, there is a ripple on the lake, and sure enough I hear the metallic tinkling of breaking ice on the

111

shore. The white and the colours brighten even more as the sun struggles through the haze of the rising mist. I look back once again at the delicate snow tracery on the trees for I know that it will all soon be shaken away. Then I draw up a log by the fire and pour a drink from my flask.

Soon there are voices as my work party approach along the lakeshore path. They sound to be in good spirits. There is a cheer as they see the fire and seven young men appear carrying axes, billhooks and saws. They lay down their tools, disburden themselves of rucksacks and coats, and are ready for work. No need to check their tools for sharpness (there is nothing more dangerous than a blunt blade). Robin, their schoolmaster leader, is bringing up the rear and he will have seen to that.

We waste no time. After the preliminary chatter we split up into two groups. Three of the lads start cutting branches and overhanging trunks under my eye, while the rest with Robin pull away the wood, cut it into manageable lengths and carry it to the fire. I have to make sure that the cuts are right. When cutting off a branch the cut must be flush with the trunk, an upward cut must be made at the base first, then a downward one to meet it, else the falling branch will tear fibres from the trunk below the cut, making an ugly wound. When felling trunks the cut must be made close to the ground too. This means bending the back to make the cut, which youngsters seem reluctant to do. I have to keep on at them or if I turn my back they start a cut a foot from the floor. I remember the biblical quotation often used by my tutor, 'The axe is laid unto the root.'

As we begin to get a good head of steam I swap over the cutting-out party. The fire now is roaring, cracking, banging and hissing away like a live thing and the heat is intense. Twigs, particularly green birch, explode like firecrackers as the branches are thrown on. And there is the rich smell of

112

birch oil, and the peppery smell of green oak and alder.

Inevitably before very long there is a climbing job as branches high up an oak sweep down to chest level. No need to ask for a volunteer; there is a squabble as to who has to go, to Robin's amusement.

'George is staying on the ground. He's just a disaster area. Mike'll go up.'

There is a cheer as Mike makes the ascent, sending down showers of snow. Once he is ensconced, someone cheerfully throws up a saw which is within an ace of taking off his ear. Several more attempts are made until a line is thrown up to him and the saw tied on the end. Most of us stop work to watch Mike as he dangles precariously from one branch and cuts away at small stuff before he can reach the branch to come off. Then he starts. I stop him and tell him he must try to get in a bottom cut. This is very difficult and he does a contortion act which would go down well at a circus. By the time I tell him that the cut will do he is panting for breath and laughing nervously at the facetious advice thrown up to him. He repositions himself, gets his breath and starts to cut.

'Your cuts are not going to meet,' I warn. 'Pull the saw over to the left.'

He starts again. It is very hard work as the wood is rock hard. Some of us get tired of watching and giving advice, and carry on working. Mike's rests become more and more frequent and he is finding his position uncomfortable, but he will not accept Robin's offer of relief. He will finish the job. Presently the limb creaks. He stops to listen then carries on. Then there is a crack and the branch descends suddenly. It hits the ground amid a shower of breaking twigs and there is a cheer. Hands grab the wood to pull it clear and cut it into smaller lengths.

We work until noon, by which time we are making

113

longer and longer journeys to the fire with our loads. Then we gather round, as I whistle, but not too close as the heat is too great, and we sit on logs and rocks to eat our sandwiches. There is some laughter as Alec discovers that he has not put his lunch in his rucksack. After a good deal of teasing we each give him a sandwich and he does rather better than the rest of us on boiled ham, chicken, egg, cheese and tomato, marmite and peanut butter. I look across the lake where the sun has lit up the white walls of Ruskin's home, now showing plainer against the dark trees behind, which have shed their snow. I look back into our wood and that too is darker where the sun and wind have touched it.

When the party begins to lark about we know that is time to restart work. We are getting on now. The cut back reveals the old track probably trodden for centuries when men cut timber for charcoal to fuel the bloomeries, the primitive iron-smelting sites along the shore. We come across the clinker from one site and find fragments of congealed liquid iron. It must have been the monks of Furness Abbey who first melted this local ore, boating it to suitable sites where there was fuel for their roughly made furnaces. I wonder if their workers shared the same high spirits as this young crew of volunteers.

By mid-afternoon we stop cutting out and concentrate on cutting up and burning. The fire is now huge, but hollow in the middle and we use long poles as pokers and levers to push the ring of unburnt material inwards. It has been dried by the heat and crackles angrily into life and we have to move back in self-defence. There is no possibility of quenching this fire before we go. We must make it safe and neat by making sure that all the fuel will be consumed and that there is no possibility of the fire site extending.

Then it is time to gather up tools and count them. There

114

have been no mishaps apart from burn holes in our old working clothes, and a few blisters. I thank the volunteers and they depart the way they came. 'Suggest another date next month,' calls Robin. I wave acknowledgement and I again have the place to myself. The lake is now lit pink and purple from the setting sun, Ruskin's home the colour of crushed blackberry. I take a last look at the fire and go back up through the wood, now in gathering gloom. The snow is still soft and silent under my tread, and lower branches untouched by sun or wind still bear their burdens now looking slightly luminous. I pick up the walking stick which I cut and hid and I stop at my birch log seat briefly and listen once more to the silence. I savour it for a moment and walk on. But before I leave the wood I stop, for something has disturbed the silence and I cannot make it out. I stand and listen and at last it comes again. It is that strange long cry that a fox sometimes makes. It is impossible to describe it as there is nothing quite like it. It is a bark with a long exhalation. In it is the essence of wildness. I stand and listen to see if he (or she) is answered. But the only answer, from away over the lake, is the cry of an owl. I let the ripples in the pool of silence fade away and I leave the wood and walk on towards the yellow lights of the village.

'Return to Base'

It is hard to believe in these days when portable radio communication is commonplace that back in the early sixties we in the mountain rescue teams were exercising our minds on the knotty problem of recalling team members after a successful search was completed, or when it was realised that we were working on a false alarm. A search could go on needlessly for hours. A typical situation was when a lone walker was reported missing overnight in the Langdale or Grasmere area and he had not left word as to where he intended going. The area of search was very large and we had a little under a hundred searchers out, split into groups, combing the likely spots. We had a base radio and only four or five hand sets. Several parties were therefore without radio contact. Around noon four of us, without radio, left search headquarters to do a rapid search of Far Easedale, above Grasmere. It was not really our lucky day.

I took my Land Rover as far as I could possibly go up the very rough and steep rocky path, and we set off, two either side of the valley, onto the ridges with binoculars. Our only signalling devices were our voices and our whistles. It was a very hard flog several hundred feet up onto the ridge,

116

especially as my unlucky partner, Stan, a veteran, was a fast walker and I had an exhausting struggle to keep up with him. I was almost on my knees when we made it. There was a cold wind on the top but the visibility was good and we could make out the tiny figures of our colleagues at the far side of the valley. We had arranged to go along the ridges of the horseshoe and meet at the centre at Greenup Edge. The ridge from Helm Crag is a deceptive up-and-downer with many hollows, a good place to get lost on, but we could only make a perfunctory search. We had to stop frequently to sweep the far valley side, and the one below us, with binoculars.

Presently Stan said, 'Do you see what I see?' I was surprised to see that he was looking at the sky to the north-west where there was a peculiar black cloud streaking down to low levels and it was moving fast in our direction.

'I don't know whether that's rain or snow coming,' said Stan, 'but we're going to get it.'

We put on waterproofs. As we felt the cold draught of the storm bearing down on us, we realised that it was not waterproofs we needed most, but crash helmets. Hailstones were hammering down on us, huge missiles, some of them like golf balls. We had to crouch on the ground, arms round our heads. The freak storm pounded at us and it really hurt. Stan was swearing and shouting with pain alternately. It seemed to go on and on. I made a protective shield from my rucksack and curled up as small as I could beneath it, but the exposed parts of my body were being hammered unmercifully. And it went on and on. It stopped very suddenly and I looked round from my shield timidly and saw that all was suddenly white. I looked at Stan. Unlike me he had not been wearing gloves and he was rubbing the backs of his hands and cursing.

'I've climbed in the Alps and the Rockies, and the

117

Himalayas, but I'm damned if I remember the likes of that before!' he exclaimed. 'I thought the end of the world had come. What on earth caused that? I reckon it's muckin' about with all those atom bombs.'

But our troubles were not over. We now found ourselves trying to walk on squashy ball-bearings. I was suddenly precipitated onto my back, looking at the cold blue sky with the wind knocked out of me. I sat upright and was about to make an appropriate remark to Stan, only to find that he was not there. I struggled to my feet and walked forward on melting hailstones the consistency and appearance of cold sago pudding. Stan had slipped some twenty feet over a bank and was trying to get upright from a prone position on his stomach, with head downhill and his feet in the air, without sliding further. He was not doing well. In an effort to be helpful and get down to him I too slipped on my side, reached him, and we found ourselves locked in a grim embrace like Cumberland and Westmorland wrestlers. Stan's mouth was only an inch or so from my ear and I got the full blast of 'What the 'ell's goin' on here!' followed by a stream of profanity. However, I was in a more favourable position with my feet below me and I dug in my toes. This was perhaps as well because Stan started to slide slowly downwards head first like an ocean liner in the first minutes of its launching from the shipyard. I bent and grabbed the hood of his anorak, and this acted as a pivot so that Stan could wriggle himself into a better position and restrain his slide. But I had slipped some way in the manoeuvres and we now found ourselves still clutching each other and struggling to get up. At this stage I noticed that Stan was making strange noises and I saw that I was clutching his binoculars' strap and slowly strangling him. Stan retaliated by heaving himself upright on my rucksack which sent me further down in another slide. But we were free and Stan, ignoring

118

my struggles to join him on my feet, was looking about him at the area of white, slowly melting to grey, and saying over and again, 'I've never seen the like.'

We staggered up to a safer position and looked across the valley. On the far side there was only a dusting of white so the storm had been very local. We started to walk on the grey slush, now rather like quicklime. Stan was on his back several times.

'These damn boot soles,' he groaned. 'Saw they were worn smooth and shot at. Shops don't stock my size. Have had new boots on order for weeks.'

I noticed then for the first time how large his feet were. I suggested he tried a skiing movement but he did not think that was very funny. But he laughed quite a bit shortly afterwards as he watched me go on my rear once again and start to toboggan downhill on my treacherously smooth waterproofs. I stopped myself by grabbing some dry bracken which promptly cut my hand. We paused to slap a dressing on it. The sun had come out quite brightly by this time and the slush was melting quickly. Then Stan cursed again. It was not his day, he groaned, the fall had done something to his binoculars and he had double vision. Eventually we were off the slippery surface and on rough ground leading down to the head of the pass at Greenup.

'What kept you?' asked Sid, who was waiting for us with his partner, when we eventually arrived. Stan told him of our bombardment, showing him the weals on the backs of his hands to prove it; he explained that he had also bruises in places he did not care to reveal. We got scant sympathy and set off down the path to search both sides of it, particularly in the ravine of the beck alongside. In better circumstances I would have enjoyed the exploration as there are some beautiful trees in the ravine, demonstrating remarkable tenacity in very thin soil. But we had to concentrate on the search and our troubles were not over.

There was a pool below me and I saw something in it which I could not identify. Dead sheep? Plastic fertiliser bag? Human body? I got hold of a branch of juniper and leaned out for a clearer view. Then the rock I was standing on collapsed. I found myself gasping for breath waist-deep in freezing water, feet scrabbling for a hold on the beck bed. I made it to the bank while Stan was laughing again and shouting a commentary on my antics to Sid and Frank. I hauled myself painfully up the bank by way of a holly bush, losing the dressing from my injured hand in the process. I tried wringing out my trousers but decided the best thing to do was to get on and bear the discomfort, and ignore Stan's hilarity. The object in the beck pool was only a discoloured rock.

But the day of misfortune was not over. I noticed at one stage that Stan was not with me. I looked back and saw that he was limping some way behind. I waited for him. 'No!' he snapped at my question, he had not had another fall, but his right boot had totally collapsed, upper parting company with sole. He had lashed all together with the lace from his rucksack. I found a piece of hemp waist line I carried at that time and we made a rather better job of the repair. Stan stuffed a sandwich in my mouth, and another in his, then opened his vacuum flask. I have seldom heard a man swear so much with his mouth full of food. The flask had broken in one of his falls. Neither of us fancied coffee laced with broken glass and mercury. Stan's progress from that point was a bit handicapped and he was definitely not in the best of moods.

'What a day!' he moaned. 'One damn thing after another.'

We eventually reached the Land Rover and drove back to search headquarters. I was sitting in soggy trousers and neither of us looked a pretty sight when we arrived. There was hardly anyone there. We had started our search at noon. The missing walker had turned up safely in Borrowdale at 12.30. The search controller apologised and said that he could do nothing as we had no radio. We had wasted some four hours on fruitless search. I thought Stan was amazingly philosophical in the circumstances.

'Well so long as the silly boogar is safe...'

The problem of recall was a serious one then and the newly formed Lake District Search and Rescue Advisory Panel decided to experiment with possible recall devices. The first attempt was organised by the police and involved setting off a very large maroon on Dunmail Raise – the nearest point to the centre of the Lake District fells. On the day of the experiment teams were dispersed about the surrounding fells and were asked to listen out and note the time when they heard the explosion, if they heard it. An enormous hole was dug in the ground where King Dunmail of Cumbria fought Edmund of Northumbria in AD 945. A steel pipe was set in it and the mortar bomb was dropped into that. The searchers were all out, straining their ears. The fuse was lit, the officials made a hurried retreat and waited. There was a massive bang, which proved beyond doubt that King Dunmail was not buried there as some believe – the noise would certainly have awakened the dead. But of the men on the hills only a handful were aware that the device had gone off – and they were on the fells directly above Dunmail. The rest were of the opinion that something had gone wrong and the device had failed to explode.

Following the failure of this experiment, Sid Cross, leader of the Langdale Rescue Team, invited everyone to come forward with new ideas. He tackled me and all I could think of was enlisting the help of the army. I called on a friend of mine who was an army major employed at a local military establishment – a gun proving ground. He offered to bring out some light weapons which he assured me made a loud noise. It was worth a try. On the day we again had searchers out, all around the Langdale fells, with instructions to note and describe anything they might see or hear and the time. Sid and his helpers were somewhat surprised to see the army vehicle arrive and the weapons set up. The experiments commenced. Each item was brought in by its demonstrator. There were rockets. Coloured flares. A klaxon hooter. A siren. Then the British army did its stuff. The major fired off several weapons and eventually produced a rather old-fashioned Bren gun and fired sustained bursts into the air.

The reports coming in at the end were varied. Some had seen a green flare. Some had seen a red parachute flair. Some had seen a rocket. Some had seen nothing. But all of them, far and wide without exception, had heard a 'machine gun'. It seemed to have gone on echoing and echoing around the central fells for many minutes.

'Right,' said Sid, 'every big search we bring in the major with his Bren gun.'

But there were more experiments. One search team member telephoned us to say that he had found the answer. It was, he told us, a device used by coastguard and lifeboat services. It was a loud maroon which fired a rocket 'hundreds of feet' into the air to let off a parachute flair. We pointed out that we had tried devices of this kind.

'Not as powerful as this bloody great monster you haven't,' he said.

On a prearranged night a number of us went down to the grounds of the college where the demonstrator taught. Unfortunately when we got to the exposed site it was blowing hard from the sea with gusts of up to force eight or nine. Some of us felt that we should call the experiment off and go to the local hostelry, but no. Was it not likely that a big search would take place in such conditions? It was. This was a very powerful rocket and the wind would not make all that difference. The man was determined to show us its worth. The device was to be fired from a firmly fixed barrel like a cannon. We stood and waited. The fuse was lit. There was a great bang and the massive rocket rose vertically some thirty feet, then, hit by a gust of wind, it turned horizontally and shot off towards the college building. There was a tinkling of glass and the viewers stood like statues, utterly spellbound. The demonstrator was looking towards the upper windows of the school, horror-stricken with his mouth open. We seemed to be waiting for some minutes then there was a very loud 'Crack! Swooooooosh –!' and one of the dormitory windows was lit up, first with a painfully dazzling white light, then changing to brilliant red. We all tore off madly towards the school, some of us, I regret to say, hampered by painful mirth. It took the contents of four fire extinguishers and a large bucket of sand to subdue the monster.

That was all a long time ago. Now there are more than enough radios to go round. They are very expensive. But when the search is complete, or it is discovered that the missing person was not on the fell at all but at some local hotel by a large fire with a pint of beer in his hand, everyone on the rain-soaked hill is told by radio at once, and can give some suitable reply.

The Right Gear

Sometimes it is hard to convince the walking public that in winter the fells can be really arctic in comparison to the easier conditions in the valleys. What look like small summit patches of snow, when viewed from below, can be very large, steep ice fields. We hear it argued that the carrying of ice axes is a new fashion encouraged by gear salesmen. In the old days of mountaineering in Britain few fell walkers carried ice axes (then 'alpenstocks'). No shepherds do. But in the old days walkers wore nailed boots and often carried sticks. Shepherds wear nailed boots and carry crooks – and in any case they will not venture out on the iced mountains except in emergencies. Nowadays only walking veterans, and cranks like myself, possess nailed boots. The moulded rubber soles worn by everyone on the hills today, while superb on rock, are useless on hard snow or ice without aid. In some conditions one must strap crampons onto such boots – wicked-looking steel plates carrying steel spikes. But the ordinary winter walker out for a day's pleasure should avoid getting into terrain where crampons are needed.

If there is snow and ice on the hills ice axes should always be carried. The snag is that while ice axes are easy to buy, instruction on their use is not generally available. Nor is good advice on the type to buy always readily given. The short axe designed for the serious ice climber is of little use to the walker. Yet one often sees walkers carrying them by the wrist strap like a handbag. A walker needs a longer shafted axe so that he can use it as a spiked walking stick, and can swing the adze end for cutting steps without bending too far and getting off balance. When used as a brake in a slide, the longer axe is at a disadvantage in a tight situation such as a gully. But an ordinary winter walker should not be messing about in an iced gully anyway.

Time and again when on patrol on ice and snow we have had to escort walkers off the hill because they had no ice axes. It is comparatively easy to climb to the summit on hard snow without an axe; it is coming down that causes difficulties. We faced a typical situation on Dollywaggon Pike. A good, wide, very well-used popular path runs below the summit of Dollywaggon to Helvellyn. In fact it is a pony track. But on this day wind-blown snow had obliterated the way and smoothed off the mountain side. The snow had started to thaw at one time and had then frozen hard. The result was a steep sheet of ice. Yet the walkers, without axes, were trying to cross it in numbers. Bryan and I could see a party of students on the line where the path should be. They were going very slowly and gingerly and as we climbed towards them we heard a girl screaming. We saw that she had slipped and was spreadeagled on her stomach with two companions hanging onto her arms. We were some distance below. Without needing to exchange a word Bryan took off towards the party while I contoured quickly along the hillside until I reached a spot directly below the girl so that I could stop her if she was let go. I was sweating at the possibility of the two holding her coming down too; I was not sure how I could deal with three of them. Having got below, I started cutting steps and making my way upwards while watching Bryan's admirable speed. But it seemed an age, with the girl still hysterical and unable to move, before he reached her, cut out some deep steps for her feet and got her upright. I joined them. When she had sufficiently recovered her composure, we cut steps and escorted the whole party back to the comparative safety of the soft snow on the south-facing slope and persuaded them to descend back into Grisedale.

One fine Easter Sunday after a considerable snowfall, virtually hundreds of poorly equipped walkers were ascending Helvellyn without axes. The Helvellyn patrol was so concerned about the dangerous state of the summit approach from Striding Edge, which was covered by a cornice, that a rope was fixed which could be used as a hand aid. The patrol expected a casualty or two. There was only one – one of the voluntary wardens. He had sugested to a man in shoes who was about to descend through the cornice that he ought to use the rope and the man turned round and said, 'Who says? I'm experienced. I know what I'm doing. You're just novices. I've just come back from the Dolomites.' Having said this the man instantly slipped onto his back, grabbed wildly for something to hang on to which happened to be the warden who had warned him, failed to get a proper hold and shot rapidly over the edge and went down with a fair turn of speed, scattering walkers on the ascent. Eventually he got up well below with no hurt except to his pride. We were so busy watching the descent that we failed to notice that the voluntary warden was cursing with pain and staring at his hand. The man had grabbed his finger before the fall – and broken it.

On another Easter Monday we spent hours helping axeless people on and off the steep portions of the frozen paths to Scafell Pike without seeing the summit. When we thought that most people were eventually returning we made the ascent to the cairn ourselves to find there a frightened woman who had tried to start a descent to the guide's route without an axe. She had slipped and cut and bruised herself on rocks, and had ascended again in fear, hoping that someone would help her down. She was not only injured, but by this time was suffering from the first stages of hypothermia. There was only a short time before nightfall and we had to help her down quickly.

Quite a number of fatalities on the winter hills could have been prevented if the victims had had ice axes and knew how to use them. When two members of a party walking in grim conditions slid to their deaths, it was revealed at the inquest that they had one or two axes with them but not enough for everyone, and that they had been warned not to go on by one of our lady voluntary wardens. They had thanked her and refused the advice.

It is easy to understand the growing resistance to buying the 'gear'. It is possible to enter a mountaineers' shop in the Lake District and walk out a great deal poorer and equipped for an ascent of the Eiger North Face. The advertisements in the outdoor magazines suggest that fell walking is a very expensive hobby indeed. And the fashions change regularly so that there is a guarantee of continuing sales. To be fair, most retailers can be trusted to give good advice. But hundreds of summer walkers are wearing boots that are far too dear, too heavy, and too stiff, the argument being that if they are good enough to tackle serious alpine climbing in arctic conditions they ought to be adequate for the British fells in summer. Light inexpensive boots, fitting well and closing firmly round the ankles to prevent the things slopping about and wearing holes in the feet, with a good well-treaded sole, are all that is needed for the average walker who has no intention of doing much walking in snow.

A simple rucksack, not too small, wind and waterproofs, a spare sweater, plenty of food, a map and compass, small first aid kit, a whistle and torch. These are the essentials. Clothing should be warm and comfortable. The rest is common sense.

Trees and Mountains

'What sort of a tree is that?' asked a visitor to the forester.

'A wooden one,' said the sweating forester who was about to fell it.

Some of the men on contract felling might merely see trees as a job of work, and that is little different to the view that a slaughterer has of his queueing line of cattle in the abattoir. When I pleaded with a land agent to spare a yew tree he accused me of being a 'tree dafty'.

'Look,' he said, 'a tree is a tree is a tree. It's a crop. You plant it. You grow it. You harvest it. You sell it.'

'The trouble is,' I told him, 'you can't see the trees for wood.'

But there is nothing that one can say to the materialist. You can ask him, 'If a living tree is only material then what is man?' but he will not be listening. 'Man is different,' he might admit if he were provoked into thought and had time to put down his pocket calculator and answer. 'Man is living flesh and blood like an animal. But he has a higher part too, an intellect.' He might even admit to a 'soul'. But then everything in nature has the material and the mystical.

Here is an oak. I cannot say whether it was planted here

by man or if an acorn fell here by chance. But it is what its environment has made it. Its root run, the depth of soil, its proximity to competition, the amount of light have determined its rate of growth. Its access to space, the direction of the falling light, exposure to the wind, the amount of natural damage determine its general shape. It is timber to a forester and a timber merchant, but it is also a sublime expression of its own situation.

A man might express himself in many ways to say in effect, 'This is how I was made. This is what I believe I am.' He can suggest it logically after self-analysis. He can say it through his work, his way of life, or attempt to express it more deeply through his art. But no writer could ever match the poetry expressed in the form of a single tree, for it speaks from its roots, through the fibres of its stem, the shape of the trunk, the turn and spread of the branches, the twisting and reaching of the twigs. A tree speaks. It speaks of a hundred summers and a hundred winters. Of storms and droughts and floods and snows, of plague and gales, of rocks and soils and hidden waters, of air and birds and pollinating insects. The whole of the message is contained in the way it has grown, precisely, to make use of what its environment has provided.

It states in essence: *'Here I am, and where I am is what I am.'*

The way of the saying can only be purely truthful. The natural laws make it impossible to lie. If a tree appears to be beautiful it is because beauty is truth and truth is beauty.

If we can spare the time to read a tree which has survived on the one spot beyond the human life-span, to a century perhaps, or even several centuries, we surely cannot remain unmoved. Primitive peoples throughout the world since time began have revered trees, and tribes in east and west have offered prayers, or asked a tree's pardon before they felled it, and they would not fell at all if its wood was not needed for their survival. To them clear-felling with chain-saws would be regarded as a horrifying obscenity. They who live close to the natural world in wilderness have an awe and respect for longevity.

If we stand back and look at how the single tree fits into the pattern of the whole of a natural wood we can see that the whole wood is a living and ever-changing conciliation of thrusting, living forms. It is a great harmony, with each taking its place. It is a balance: a scheme for existence wholly constituted by the laws of nature and it can only be perfect.

If we stand back even further and see how this wood fits into the natural landscape (for at this distance human intrusions and influence are mere scratches and blemishes on the surface), then we can marvel even more as to how each piece conforms with the lake stretching out below, and behind, the mountains.

The mountains! Everything in nature has the material and the mystical. What can one say of mountains? Here is a mountain. It is not just a massive heap of worn and broken rock debris left by chance. It has been thrust upwards by the enormous heat-generating pressures from the lateral movement of the earth's crust, and from the moment of its fiery ascent the forces of the elements have clawed away at its surface. Great rivers of moving ice have cut it and undermined it. Alternate heat and frost have shattered it. Endless rains have gullied it and great rivers, loaded with debris, have scoured its feet. So slowly that the change is missed by human perception, the inexhaustible process continues. A mountain stands in cold, hard, inanimate silence, wrinkled with the wisdom of a million years and pointing to the sky.

It is the overawing sense of the huge scale of this

monument to birth and destruction and the colossal and immeasurable forces of nature of which it speaks that can draw men to the mountain. It gives a new and more realistic perspective from which to see the petty human predicament and its daily preoccupations. But there is more than that in the hypnotic fascination of mountains. That in man which responds to the sublime is captivated by the sublime beauty of mountains. The dedicated mountaineer is drawn inexorably to the peaks. It is a sort of sickness that defies pathology. A 'hard-man' climber might scoff at the suggestion that there is anything mystical in the attraction, but he would most likely be lying. During an argument at a meeting of mountaineers about damage done by hard climbers to a particular crag climbed without the land owner's permission, one of the 'hard men' who had been using the crag argued angrily, 'No person can own anything like that. It belongs to God.' Ask a climber, fell walker, or mountaineer about the attraction of mountains and he might be stumped and embarrassed. The answer 'because it is there' is feebly inadequate. It has been a sick joke for many, many years. How can one explain what is wholly mystical to the man who can only see the outward form?

We humans have hardly begun to understand where we are, who we are, and why we are. In the tree, the forest, the landscape and the mountain there is no mistake. There is the natural law which binds every unique individual component. If civilised man pretends that he can live outside the natural law, he is indulging in suicidal delusion. We cannot afford to be cynically materialistic. Nature and the natural landscape have something to say to us about living. We need to read and listen.

Pedestrian Precinct

There are conferences, lectures, courses, interviews that take me to the town and here I am on one of these visits with time to kill. It is evening. The pedestrian precinct of the town shopping-centre is empty and the commuters gone home. The shops have closed and I walk alone past the shop windows: transistor radios, televisions, furniture, the butchers and the bakers, two supermarkets. All quiet, and I am instantly enthralled by the song of a blackbird – sweet, plaintive, dragging out each phrase to a soft heart-tearing conclusion, and pausing for effect.

Then on again, echoing through the streets and the hollow arcades, with the sweet, sweet statement, quietening to another pause. I cannot tell where he is. In the old sycamore perhaps in the square at the street's end, or on some wall corner, or in some civic plantation of flowering cherries down some turning. But he has a lone heart-stirring song which pulls me away from the idle stare at the 'Special offer! Limited period only', and the 'Buy now while stocks last!' to green thoughts of woodlands where the pleasures are all free and undemanding. He sings on as if he is enjoying his sweet bliss of solitude. Another pause, and

133

then another phrase pouring on to a subdued sad ending, and another pause. There is no challenging answer to his song, nothing but the distant sound of traffic and my own footsteps.

It is the single song that stirs the heart. The nightingale would not sound so sweet if his voice broke through the chorus of the day songs. It is the single song in the waiting silence that moves the world. It is as blissful as a cool, kind hand on a fevered forehead. I wait and listen again as he goes on to each interval, each one long enough to stimulate an agonising demand for more and more of his delicious outpouring. The gold-billed bird with the silver throat has made the concrete jungle into an Eden. I was enjoying the town, the bustle, the company, the evening lights in the windows, but now he has reminded me of each creature's utter loneliness. Even as we move among the crowd we carry with us the deep dark well of our personal solitude.

Hardknott

Every weekend hundreds of motorists grind their cars up the one-in-three-and-a-half steepness and hairpin bends of Hardknott Pass. It is a painful process as the road is narrow with passing-places and there are regular gear-torturing and clutch-burning traffic jams. The vast majority of the motorists have no idea that they are negotiating passes which were engineered by the Romans over eighteen hundred years ago. This was the tenth Iter, a supply road linking the fort of Ambleside and the fort and port of Ravenglass. Before ascending Hardknott, the road had to climb Wrynose Pass from Little Langdale. For seven miles the Roman engineers had to hack and build their way through some of the roughest land in Britain, twice climbing to over twelve hundred feet. In parts this must have been an ancient British way over which the trade in stone axes passed, but the Roman improvements included on the approach to Hardknott Pass summit a cutting fifteen feet deep, and as much wide, through the base of Raven Crag. The Roman road had to make use of terracing, cutting, and had to put in many curves with only brief straight alignments. The modern road does not follow the Roman line all the way, but the Romans were the pioneers.

Nor are many motorists aware that on the descent to Eskdale, perched on the fell side to their right are the ruins of a Roman fort built on the most dramatic site in Britain, with views northward to the highest land in England, and westwards to the sea. It is perched on an airy ledge, with the bath-house below on the approach road, and a great flat parade ground has been cut and cleared out of the mountain side above. The fort guarded this important supply road, one of the many which crossed the country like rungs in a ladder.

There was a number of cars parked, on the fine spring day, in the lay-by below the fort. I parked the Land Rover and walked up. There were groups of people walking within the fort's granite walls, examining the stone foundations of the granary and the headquarters building. Much of the stone was robbed by the cartload for building, early in this and late in the last century, but some of the broken walls have been put back up by the Department of the Environment and it is pleasing to be able to see the form and shape of the fort without difficulty. Fragments of an inscribed stone of slate, which must have been carted over the steep passes from Langdale, were removed to a museum. Its original inscription is assumed to have read: 'For the Emperor Caesar Trajan Hadrian Augustus, son of the divine Trajan, Conqueror of Parthia, grandson of the divine Nerva, Pontifex Maximus, thrice consul, the Fourth Cohort of Dalmations.' What must they have thought of this place, these men from the shores of the warm Adriatic, who had walked the long weary endless miles across Europe to end up here rebuilding a ruined fort perched on the side of a mountain and open to the wet Atlantic storms? Like all veteran campaigners perhaps they had already come to the view that one place was much like another and that one can only make the best of things, stick it out and hope for an early return home.

I remember in the navy hearing for the first time the stock reply of my veteran leading-hand when we went ashore in Gibraltar after flogging through the worst storm, it was said, for many years. When he was asked by a man at the bar what ship we came off he just said grimly, 'Hardship.'

'It is very interesting here,' one of my friends wrote home. 'The other day I saw the place where Christ was born,' and then he added: 'I wish to Christ I was where I was born.'

Once I was battened below decks at my post not knowing what was happening in the intense gunnery noise above. After we had stood down and I returned to the mess I asked my chief PO what had been going on, and he replied in his broad lowland Scots, 'Well laddie, it was a bit like the Dumbarton Arms on a Saturday night when Celtic beat the Rangers one nil after a disputed penalty.' It is the grim ironical acceptance of all that comes as if it were commonplace that marks the veteran. I can picture the weary Dalmatians tramping painfully over the pass and looking down at the rain sodden ruin that was to be their back-breaking task and their home, to hear their *principalis* calling, 'There it is, lads, Mediobogdum, the lap of luxury! Now don't go breaking into a run. We'll be there soon enough.'

As I walked towards the north gate with its dramatic view to the central fells, there was an unusually good father explaining to his very small daughter how the fort was organised.

'But why,' I heard her ask, 'did they have to go to war?'

I did not hear his answer, but as I sat on the knoll beyond the wall looking down deep into the green valley to where

137

the Roman road once stretched to the port of Ravenglass, I wondered how I would have answered her. Because of the greed and ambition of politicians? Perhaps to fulfil an altruistic need to 'put things right', to create order among the chaos of tribal feuds? But for the men themselves, eager to return to the warm blue sea and the hills of home, they were brought here to do a job for reward. And they might like the uncertainty, the risk, the challenge to some extent. Then there are the basics: the pack instinct, the hatred and fear of the unknown, the involuntary black hot violent response. But a child could not understand these important things. One could only answer, 'Because men are foolish.' Then this great stone fort built from sweat and blood and hardship, set on this impossible ledge, is a monument to human folly? And if I said that, I could maybe imagine the Dalmatian ghosts smiling grimly and nodding agreement. The long weary lengths to which men will go to act out their pitiful comedy!

I was disturbed from my reverie by a family.

'Why,' asked the father, 'did they make a gateway here which leads nowhere?' He looked nervously over the cliff.

'I suppose,' I said, 'that every Roman fort had to have four gates, one in the centre of each wall. It was down in standing orders?'

I offered to lead them to the parade ground and they followed me as I picked my way through the boggy land above the fort (Mediobogdum *sounds* as if it was well named). They gasped in amazement when we got there, for the scenery around is positively ferocious. Crags jutt from the steep slopes which fall down to the hollows of the valley far below, and everywhere there are boulders, great fields of scattered boulders, the debris of glaciation. Yet here is a large flat green square dug out of the hillside and complete-ly clear of stone with a dais where the commander would take the salute. No doubt it was built with slave labour, but in an environment hostile to neat order, it is an engineering triumph. And made just so that men could march up and down to someone's command? There would be games too, with a bit of gambling on the side, to relieve the boredom of stern Roman duty.

The hundreds of motorists grind by, most of them unaware of the existence of the Roman fort, and perhaps not interested if they did know. For Hardknott Pass, once sweated over by the Romans, is now the motorists' great challenge. For the road is one of the steepest in Britain with fierce hairpins, reaching 1291 feet at its top. Furthermore, it can only be reached (unless one takes a wide diversion through Dunnerdale) by taking in another challenging pass, Wrynose (the pass of the Stallion), 1281 feet, which does not have as many hairpins. Both roads are narrow with passing places, and there's the rub. In theory descending motorists should give way to ascending, but sometimes motorists meet between passing places, or someone refuses to give way, or a vehicle decides it cannot make it and grinds to a stop. Then the jams start and sometimes the roads can be snarled up for an hour or more. When I had to deal with an accident to a motorcyclist at Wrynose Bottom, between the two passes, it took an hour and a half for an ambulance to reach us. A lot of the mishaps are due to bad driving. Motorists cannot believe that they can only negoti-ate some of the steep bends by dropping to bottom gear; they try to make it in second. Clutch failures, and brake failures, are common, and now and then a car loses the road and drops off the edge. Miraculously there are no fatalities. Perhaps the Roman gods still keep a guardian's eye on travellers here.

There used to be an elderly motorist, with a well-kept 1930s car reguarly parked in a lay-by part way up Hardknott on the Wrynose side. It is well sited for a view of the first ferocious hairpin and the man was there on many Sundays watching drivers make a hash of their attempts at the frightening angle and turn. I would stop with him for a while.

'For entertainment,' he said, 'this beats television.'

He would puff at his pipe and when a car was approaching occasionally he would take the pipe out of his mouth and smile.

'This man thinks he can make it in second gear. Watch this!'

Sure enough the car would stop dead on the formidable incline. Before the driver could get away again he had to reverse down and round the hairpin to more level ground. If there was another motorist close on his tail this meant there was more fun as both cars had to reverse and more might be banking up behind them. Some motorists find reversing very difficult even on level ground. This happened time and time again. Other motorists, having failed in second gear, would have another try still in second after gaining momentum with a run. The result was inevitable. On one occasion, as I watched, a car was followed far too closely by a bunch of motorcyclists. The car stalled and the motorcyclists unable to overtake had to stop too. One or two of the bunch could not hold their heavy bikes on the incline. So bikes were ditched and the heavier ones had to be manhandled by several men sweating in their leathers. The result was chaos with bikes everywhere and petrol leaking onto the road to add to the excitement.

I was climbing above the same spot in the Land Rover one day and saw a saloon car coming down towards me quite fast – backwards. I managed to drive onto a narrow patch of grass as the car swept past. I jumped out of my vehicle and ran down after the car, expecting a crash at any moment. Miraculously he steered round the bends and managed to pull up in a passing place on the lower level. I went down to the driver. He was quite green. His wife was white and terrified too. So were mother and father-in-law and junior on the back seat. Even the family dog looked frightened. I do not know why but I asked if I could help. He looked at me with his eyes still wide with terror.

'Stalled,' he gasped, 'And the hand-b-b-b-brake wouldn't hold.' He breathed heavily for a time, then turned to me appealingly. 'C-c-could you t-tell me the way to B-B-Blackpool?'

A relative of mine, who is an electrical engineer and who loves the Lake District, was approached by a colleague who asked him the best route to Calder Hall, the atomic power station, as he had to do a job there and had not been before. My relative enthused about the Lake District and suggested that he did the job on the Friday, took his wife with him, dropped her off at Ambleside at a hotel, went to West Cumberland to do the job, then joined his wife for a weekend in the Lakes. And this is what he did. However the main road journey to Calder Hall from Ambleside is a longish, tortuous journey through Keswick, then going west, and south by the Whitehaven by-pass. When he had finished the job it was dark and it was raining. He asked one of the workmen if there was a shorter way back to Ambleside.

'Aye,' he said, 'Over t' passes.' And the workman explained how to find Eskdale for the start of the journey.

He described the epic journey afterwards. He went up the dark valley of Eskdale with only a glimmer of light here and there as he passed solitary farms. The rain pelted down and his headlights could only probe a few yards ahead. As he approached and climbed what he later was told was Hardknott Pass visibility got even worse as he got into the cloud. The road turned suddenly one way and then the other. The bends came at him without warning so that he was wrestling madly with the wheel to avoid the banks. Then the climb started in earnest, so steep that he could not believe it. He was thrust back in his seat and as he concentrated on giving the engine full revs he suddenly found himself fighting the mad bends, not daring to slacken speed lest he ground to a stop. The ordeal seemed to go on and on impossibly with the engine screaming all the time. 'Surely no more,' he thought, yet, he said, more and more of them kept coming at him. Suddenly to his relief the road levelled as he crossed the summit. Then he approached the descent. The road took a mad dive and he was poised on its brink. The headlights were just shining into space and he could see no road at all. He stopped. He cursed because he had no torch, and went out into the rain with his cigarette lighter searching for the road in front. When he realised it plunged downwards he crossed himself and got back in the car and eased it forward. He went down in first gear; even so, he swore he was jumping on his brake and battling with his wheel round impossible bends. Eventually he reached the bottom of the pass and mumbling gratitude for safe deliverance he drove on. But then came Wrynose Pass.

Once again he found himself going up what he thought was an impossible road. He crossed yet another summit and once again found his headlights shining out into space. This time he edged forward with a muttered prayer and found himself descending a madly angled concrete ramp. At last he was at the foot of the pass and on a narrow twisting undulating road. Eventually he reached Ambleside and the hotel.

'What's the matter?' asked his wife. 'You look as if you've seen a ghost!'

'I'll tell you,' he stammered, 'but right now I want two or

maybe three double gins.'

The road is banned to heavy vehicles. However, one day Mike, a voluntary warden, and I, were high on the fell above Wrynose when we saw a strange vehicle far below us climbing the pass. It looked like a huge square box, and not having binoculars at the time we could not make anything of it. Some time later we were able to descend to satisfy our curiosity. Then we saw the problem. A large lorry had attempted to climb the pass (the driver said he missed the prohibition sign at the foot) and when the vehicle had failed to make it he had reversed. Unfortunately his nearside wheels got too close to the edge and the roadside crumbled under the weight. So it was half on and half off the road and poised over a deep drop. The lorry was loaded with barrels of wine and it was difficult to imagine how it could be unloaded. The large square vehicle we had seen climbing the pass was a heavy-recovery vehicle with large chunky wheels, a crane and a great winch. When we approached them there was a massive steel hawser from the winch, round a boulder about the size of a garden shed above the road, and back to the lorry. The winch was started and the cable began to wind onto the drum. But strangely the lorry was not moving. Then Mike gasped and pointed at the boulder. It was gradually being winched down the hill towards us, digging out a great trench as it came. Another moment and it might have started to roll. We stopped the operation, and there was a tense silence for a while. We eventually got the lorry back onto the road by winching its weight onto the wheels already on the macadam and building up under the poised wheels with rocks. It took a long time.

'I've been here nearly all day,' the lorry driver groaned. 'Lord knows what the office are going to say.' His troubles were not over. A police car came winding up the hill. As we left we saw that the officer had his notebook out and was saying, 'I'm going to have to report you for driving on a restricted road. You have blocked the pass nearly all day.' Luckily it was a quiet mid-week day.

It is common to see cars being pushed on the passes, sometimes by unlikely helpers while the driver sits tight with his foot hard down and praying hard that he will make the next level – pretty girls in fashion boots and summer frocks, stout aunts in furs, whole families all pushing, sometimes joined by passing walkers, and other motorists who want to clear a way for their own cars. The road is stained by rusty water from boiling radiators, the few places where there are grass verges are rutted from wheel-spin, and there is a general scattering of stones which have been used as chocks. On both sides of the passes the local break-down services make a little bit of weekend profit. It must be a trade as old as history. The Roman supply waggons must have had problems too.

Working Dogs

It is a joy to see good sheep dogs working a flock. The rapport between the shepherd and his dog is uncanny. Running a hill farm without dogs would be quite impossible. With good animals life is so much easier. A farmer friend told me that he was once gathering the flock into his pen and he said aloud in front of Jacky, his older dog, 'We've dropped ten somewheres.' When he went to feed his dogs Jacky was missing. He saw him on the fell an hour later – bringing in the lost ten.

Over pints at the local though, stories about clever dogs get a bit tall. At one session I noticed that Charles, a man who did know something about breeding and training sheepdogs, was remarkably quiet.

'You've bred some clever dogs in your time?' I ventured.

'Oh aye.'

'Which do you reckon was your best?'

He thought for a moment.

'Well this Scotsman came and said he wanted a goodun. A good few years back it was. He was offerin' a hoondred punds which was a lot of brass in them days. But he wanted summat special. An' he was ready to wait. Well I bred from

145

two gooduns – Flash – a brilliant dog which would a' fillt oose wi' gowd cups if I'd used im in trials. An t' bitch was Nell, cleverest bitch in t' coontry I reckoned. Well I giv him pick o' t' litter. That dog was bringin in ducks from t' pond when it was eight weeks owd, an' it could count up to eleven.'

I looked closely at Charles but he looked dead serious.

'Aye he was pleased as poonch an' off he went wi' it.'

'Did you hear how he went on?'

'Oh aye. A year later.'

'How?'

'Well 'is wife comes roarin' into t' yard playin 'ell.'

'Why?'

'Well. She couldn't do owt wi' er oosband. He'd gone as thin as a whippet.'

'Why?'

Charles took his time and pulled slowly at his pint.

'Well, John, it seems that this dog was so bloody clever, within twelve moonths it had got t' job sorted oot. The dog was doin' t' whistlin' an' t' Scotsman was doin't runnin'.'

I have always had a dog, not always from choice because they have been given to me, but I have usually managed to establish a good relationship. A dog can be very useful to a warden. Good training needs some dedication and time. Claife is my second German shepherd dog and the rapport is close. Although she is strong-willed and sometimes slow, she responds to commands whether shouts, whistles, a hissing, or a hand signal. At an early stage I taught her to find objects I had thrown aside when she was not looking. This proves useful as I am always leaving things behind on some job or other and she can smell them out. To her it is a great game. She was little more than a year old when I was walking off a crag top after taking a photograph. As I descended I noticed that Claife was hanging back with her mouth open and her tail wagging. I called her in, she made a few steps forward and hung back again.

'What's the matter with you?' I called, and she looked puzzled at my anger.

When I began to move back towards her she started up the path to the crag. I ran and she broke into a run too. I was mystified at this behaviour and when I got back to the crag she was sitting there, her mouth open and her tail wagging furiously. At her feet was my light-meter, just where I had forgotten it. The dog must have seen me put it down and thought that we were playing her favourite game.

At two years old she was attending mountain search classes with me. A mountain search dog is taught, not to follow a ground scent, but to 'home in' on human air scent. The reason is obvious. If someone is lost on a mountain he could be lying injured for hours after his ground scent was gone. The first exercise therefore is simple. Someone holds your dog and you run away. When out of sight of the dog you turn at an angle and circle back, then hide. The dog, frantic with worry, is let loose on the command 'Seek!' or 'Find!'. It races off in the direction you first went, but should check and short-cut to your hiding place when it picks up your scent drifting on the air. You make a fuss of the dog and show it that it is a great game. The second exercise is the same, but this time a stranger runs off with you and shares the hiding place. When the dog finds, both you and the stranger praise it. For the third exercise you hold the dog while the stranger runs off to hide. Then you give the command 'Seek!' let her loose, and follow her. Over a long period the exercise is done on varying terrain in all weathers, during the day, and in the darkness.

Most of the dogs love searching in snow. For this exercise you need some fearless volunteers who are prepared to be buried in a deep grave in the snow. Most of the volunteers prefer to climb into a large plastic bag before the snow is shovelled onto them. They need to be left an air pocket and a ventilation hole. Usually there is no problem in the finding. There is no extraneous scent to put dogs off. What is surprising is that scent can penetrate through to the surface. In the Alps dogs have picked up scent coming from great depths after avalanches. The first snow exercise is usually the basic one. Another handler holds your dog while you go off and get yourself buried at various depths. My first four-foot one was quite an experience. I found myself pinned down with what seemed like a ton of snow which a colleague was gaily and enthusiastically shovelling, and patting down firmly. He pulled out the ice axe which had been planted with me, leaving, he hoped, a thin shaft of ventilation. He covered his tracks with the spade as he left. The wait seemed endless. I concluded that someone had tied my dog up, that everyone had forgotten me and gone off down to the valley to the pub. My arms were pinned down helplessly. Just as I was fighting back some panic there was a noise like thunder above my head. I was then aware of movement there. A patch of pale light became evident. There was a flickering shadow and my ventilation shaft was blocked. Then there was a burst of light, a draft of air, a snorting noise, and a great black paw was digging furiously towards my face. I had been warned to hold my hands firmly in front of my face and I saw why. Great teeth reached down and grabbed my hand. My dog was trying to pull me out! I tried to shout and in self-defence I had to let her take my glove. The ridiculous animal then went away with it. I was told later that onlookers were amused as she started playing with my glove until someone kindly thought of commanding her to 'Seek' again. She moved back to my grave, dug in again and I had to offer her my other glove. This time she had removed enough snow to free my face

148

and I was able to shout and tell her what I thought of her. She then came back obligingly and with her furious and highly dangerous help, I was able to get my arms free.

In training, the handler has more to learn than the dog. The dog is only doing what comes naturally. You have to understand that she is receiving messages through her nose all the time. You have to read her reactions. Once the dog knows you are interested in what she is doing she is only too willing to communicate. It is up to you to try to understand. So you miss no opportunity to praise her when she reveals to you such treasures as a dead frog, an inhabited rabbit hole, a bird's feather. You should show interest in everything so that it becomes second nature.

'What is it Claife?' I asked my dog as I clambered somewhat wearily to the summit ridge of a high Scottish mountain. Her ears had gone up and she had looked at me and she was staring over the side. I caught up with her and followed her gaze downwards. I dropped to my knees. My stomach turned as I realised unexpectedly that she was staring down a fifteen hundred feet vertical cliff. When I had composed myself and looked again, I could see a herd of red deer in the glen far below.

It would be grand to say that Claife had done a dramatic life-saving find. But in every search, exercises apart, we have always been on the wrong part of the mountain. However, there have been one or two time-saving jobs. We had just reached the end of Striding Edge one wet and foggy Sunday afternoon when I met a frightened couple.

'Someone has fallen off the edge' said the man, 'We feel certain. We heard someone scream.'

'Where abouts?'

'Towards the 'bad step'.'

'Which side did they fall down?'

'I don't know. We just heard this scream and then we

heard a man shout!'

I took Claife by the collar, looked at her and shouted 'Seek!'

She was off along the edge in front of me and instantly disappeared. I used my pocket radio to warn some voluntary wardens in a work party in the valley far below to stand by, and hurried after my dog.

I continued for some time, concentrating on putting my feet down safely. There was no sign of Claife. I called her back. She came eventually out of the mist, her tongue out and her tail up.

'Have you found?' I asked, 'Go on. Show me!'

She was off again, and again she had vanished. After more struggle I called her back again. She came in once more, obviously in a state of excitement. We repeated this procedure until at last she returned to me, not from the edge, but from below.

'Show me!' I called and picked my way through the crags after her.

I eventually saw her below in the mist where she was sitting next to a boy who was on his feet. It was only when I descended further that I saw that a man was lying by the boy's side. He was elderly and he was white with pain and groaning through his teeth. I made sure that he was perched safely and examined his head. No injury at all. I asked where he was injured.

'Body and legs.'

I unzipped his anorak and ran my fingers down his back. He winced a bit but there was, I thought, nothing worse than bruises. He shouted when I felt his ribs. There were either bad bruises there or fractures. He was breathing reasonably. On examination both legs seemed all right and he was able to move them. In fact he had suffered only cracked ribs and bruising and we marvelled at his luck.

After a rest he was able to clamber back with aid, to the edge, and then slowly and painfully along it. I could then radio down for help. He was a tough man who had been walking for years. The accident was caused when he had caught a foot in his waterproof over-trousers and tripped. He had gone about seventy feet and had bounced and scraped down, expecting he said, to have his brains knocked out at any second. Claife's 'find' certainly saved time in searching, and contributed to the man's morale.

On another I was at Stickle Tarn at the end of an afternoon when all the world seemed to have been pounding up the Stickle Ghyll track. I was talking to a group of late arrivals when I noticed to my horror that an extremely large woman had reached the tarn. She was covered in perspiration, was near exhaustion, and she was wearing sandals. I thought to myself 'If she breaks her leg I don't think I want to be around.' The prospect of carrying such a huge load was terrifying. However, there was a lot going on around the tarn as people were beginning to leave and head down again. For a time I forgot the large lady and it was only when Claife and I were beginning our descent that my conscience gave a small twinge. 'Accidents always happen on the way down.' I thought, 'Best see how she's getting on.'

But I could not see her anywhere below, among the moving groups. Part way down I began to think that she could not possibly have got out of sight so fast, so I looked at Claife and called 'Seek!' She was off downwards gaily. I could see her moving around the rocks now and then on both sides of the path when I was not concentrating on my own descent. Then I realised that she was not in sight and was obviously not moving about and searching. I could only conclude that she had 'found'. What had she found? Difficulty was that there was so much human scent around.

In these circumstances the exercises had taught her that the 'casualty' was the person who was lying down and hiding. As she was not searching she had obviously sat down by someone who was reclining. It could be someone having a rest. It could be a courting couple (in which case I would have to apologise). Or more probably it could be someone taking refreshment, for Claife is a born scrounger. It was none of these. She came over to me, tail wagging, from a man who was sitting with his back to a rock. He had just suffered a heart attack. As it happened a companion had run down to call out the rescue team, but without Claife's help I would certainly have walked past him. In the event I was able to make him comfortable and keep up his morale. When the rescue team appeared I was able to signal our position and speed their approach. The story has a happy ending. We called in an RAF rescue helicopter as he was too poorly to carry. He was soon in hospital and he eventually made a good recovery.

The third occasion was rather bizarre. We had come down into Langdale from Stickle Tarn when the landlord at the hotel told me that the rescue team had been called out. There was a man with a badly cut leg somewhere near the top of the ghyll, he said.

But I've just come down from there' I exclaimed. 'I saw no one.'

'I can only tell you what I've been told. I've called out the team.' I put my rucksack back on, took the long doglead, put it over my shoulder, and clipped the ends together, and set off up the hill again. Claife was puzzled but delighted. Part way up a man came down with very bad news.

'Are you on your way to the casualty?' he asked.

'Yes'

'That's quick work. My mate's only just gone down to call the team! It's a bad gash and he has arterial bleeding.

I've put two tourniquets on his leg.'

Two tourniquets! I wondered how long I had got to reach him. I put on a burst of speed. Tourniquets can do some nasty damage. Wrongly placed they can make bleeding worse. We still had only vague directions so I told Claife to 'Seek. hup – hup!' She ran on ahead. By the waterfall at the top she moved off to the left. I followed her with my eye as I struggled on and was able to take a short cut in her direction. This saved some effort and time. Soon afterwards she came down to me again, hovered in front, and was clearly saying 'Come on! Why are you so slow?' She rushed back and stopped at a group of people above. As I approached I could see that they were sitting round a man who lay on the ground. They appeared to be waiting for his leg to drop off. I arrived at last, covered in sweat and gasping for breath with the eyes of the public on me. They were waiting for action. There was a bit of blood around. The casualty was white and shocked but not bleeding profusely. I slipped the rucksack off my shoulder and brought it round to the front to get out the first aid kit. Unfortunately I had forgotten about the dog lead which I had slung above the sack straps. The lead was tangled, one end came out with the sack, the other tightened like a noose round my neck. In the confusion I did not know what to do and the crowd appeared to watch in fascination. Disappointed at not seeing a man's leg fall off they were about to witness a slow strangulation.

But this story had a happy ending too. I released myself. Watched approvingly by Claife who was sitting dutifully by the casualty, I elevated the man's leg, cut off the tourniquets in spite of protests from spectators, and placed a padding and a firm bandage over the man's wound. Half an hour later he was in the hands of the stretcher party.

There was a promising moment of glory when Claife was

153

a television star. It could have been impressive. It was not. The camera team wanted a shot of dogs finding a 'casualty' in snow. The cameraman had a bright idea. He would sit in a snow hole and film a dog actually finding him. The producer decided that he wanted a handsome alsation as they looked more impressive than the other breeds we were using. Claife's moment had come. The cameraman took up his position. Action! I told Claife to seek. It had been a hard day but she seemed willing and alert. She curved off widely and then checked dramatically as she caught the air scent. She moved in fast right up to the cameraman. Not liking the look of the man with the strange contraption on his shoulder, she barked – which was even more impressive. Unfortunately there was something wrong with the camera and we would have to do it again. I took Claife back. Action! I told her to seek and she was off but this time she was casual. She knew where the man was and she was in no hurry. In spite of my frantic shouts to arouse her excitement she sauntered slowly up to the camera and sneered into the lens, adding a look of extreme boredom. It was this film that was shown in a million homes. Search dogs in action! It was humiliating.

Claife's work is normally prosaic. She is an eager companion. She is sedate and elderly, but she can do mundane jobs like watching my property. She finds objects. She shows me people or tents on apparently empty fell. She can tell me if a piece of litter has been dropped by the person standing near it. She is a talking point and makes no objection if small children throw their arms around her. She recovers objects from the lake shallows. She barks on command which is sometimes useful if you want to attract someone's attention. She has even proved a help in surveying work. I was helping a Planning Officer mark out a boundary line to some woodland that the National Park had

154

just acquired. We had the poles, but the boundary went through shoulder-high bracken and it was raining. We found the line we had to walk on and planted the markers as we went along. Unfortunately at the far end of the boundary we looked back and we could see nothing of the markers in the high bracken and swirling rain. We needed to walk back along the line to fix the position of another boundary. How to do it? I told Claife to seek. She picked out the markers one by one, sitting dutifully by each until we joined her. She was playing her favourite game.

Three Tarns

I have gained this height against a wind saturated by rain. There is nothing familiar about the crags in front of me. Usually I see them all crouching shoulder to shoulder like rugby players in a scrum. Now I come across them in the boiling mist one at a time and they are like cold hooks of steel thrusting suddenly into my vision, clawing sharply upwards as if they are trying to tear out the entrails of the storm. Through the noise of wind and rain beating at my anorak hood there is the sound of falling torrents. What can be a friendly place is now an angry brawling battleground between wind and rain and rock, and I am an intruder caught in the cross-fire. The path is a stream.

'Have you ever thought, on the hill in trying conditions,' asked a keen mountaineering friend 'What the hell am I doing here? I could be at home in an armchair with a good book.'

Precisely. But I have arranged to patrol, and to meet up with another patrol from Bowfell, at Three Tarns.

Gaining the ridge of Crinkle Crags, in spite of the appalling weather, I keep coming across saturated walkers walking crab-wise towards me to take the squalls on their shoulders. I look at all of them and shout cheery things like, 'Do you think it's going to rain?' Presently there comes along a family in plastic raincoats looking worried.

'Which way to Langdale?'

I look at the children; one in early teens is white and cold. I offer them sweets and they tell me they are lost. No compass. I explain that they have to keep the wind on their right shoulder and in about fifteen minutes they should see the path turning left, they should then have the wind behind them on a good path to Red Tarn where they should turn left again.

'We took the wrong path once.'

I tell them a compass is a good idea and show them mine and recommend that they buy the same kind. I press on.

'Have you seen a dog – a black mongrel?' shouts the next walker against the noise of the wind. An anxious elderly man, obviously tired.

'Where's your car?'

'Wrynose.'

'You could go down there. I'll bet it's got fed up with the weather and it's waiting for you there.'

I ask him his name and where he is staying and pencil the information in my notebook.

'If I find it I'll try to catch it and bring it down and let you know. But I'd get off the mountain. I'll bet the dog has. It's too bad to hang about!'

Twenty minutes later I am at Three Tarns at the end of the ridge and get the full blast of the wind tearing up from Lingcove. I look at my watch. There is no sign of Ron in the racing mist, but there is a group of four young men with large rucksacks. 'Duke of Edinburgh's Award expedition,' they shout in answer to my question. They are heading for lower Eskdale. We crowd round a map and I try to show them how they must avoid finishing in Moasdale. They wave and head on into the teeth of the storm. Ron arrives from the direction of Bowfell with a party of children with one youth leader. He gives me a meaningful look, his eyes shining with anger, and I take in the party's motley footwear and their soaked jeans. The leader looks very unhappy as without doubt he has already had a discussion with Ron about why he is up there with children on a day like this. No need for me to speak at all. I just look at him and he turns away. We see them down onto the Band heading for Langdale's head, then sit in the lee of a crag and open flasks.

'There was an army youth camp at Angle Tarn,' reports Ron, his mouth close to my ear. 'They were leaving though and I stayed and watched them off. Twenty-five on Bowfell apart from this school group. Some of them lost for a way off. They all cleared O.K.'

He stretches out on the wet grass as if he were on a settee in a comfortable parlour and pours some tea. The wind is howling through the gap in the hills like a banshee and I drop down with Ron to find myself in that pool of relative stillness below the incline of rushing air. Someone's map flies over our heads, flapping like a crow in the wind and vanishing rapidly in the mist in the direction of Langdale. A party of three, well equipped, and well loaded, flop down beside us.

'We planned to camp here!' one shouts. 'We've just decided not to bother!'

'Where were you heading after that?'

'General direction of Wasdale.'

I bring out my map carefully folded open and held tight and advise them to get down into Lingcove and find a sheltered place there.

'You may have to drop a thousand feet to Throstle Garth area.'

They nod agreement.

'We'll make for Wasdale tomorrow from there.' They grin, give a thumbs up sign, drag themselves to their feet and fight their way into the gale.

We debate what to do next. Ordinarily we would have had a good look at the Three Tarns area, pick up any litter, and then split up. But today we had better have a mind to mountain safety and go together along Crinkle Crags. If anyone is going to go astray it will be on that ridge. There is also the matter of the missing dog. We pick ourselves up, have a last look round and push on up the end of the ridge, or where it should be if we could see it. We struggle up for about ten minutes and I see a fearsome looking pinnacle ahead which should not be there. (Am I on the Coolin on Skye?) Closer encounter shows it to be a far more modest peak than the mist deceived us into believing. We struggle on without conversation for some time. Fifteen minutes after the peak we meet with a well-equipped but worried couple.

'We're trying to get down to Langdale,' the man shouts. 'We took a wrong turning once and found ourselves down towards Wrynose.'

'That's not unusual. Come with us.' A thought occurs to me. 'Did you see a dog heading in that direction?'

No, they have not. We battle on. Rain has found its way at long last past the barrier of my towelling scarf. Ron hands round chocolate pieces. I take the lead, leaning on the wind and peering for the route ahead, staggering as the wind lets go in the lee of sheltering rocks, or hits us as it comes swirling round at new angles. Some of the big blasts pick up small stones from around the path and carry grass clumps torn off the fell below. Sometimes the wind noise as it pulls at my anorak hood is so unpleasantly loud that I have to turn my head, or clap gloves over ears. Presently we are descending the 'bad step', a minor scramble and we are struggling down to Red Tarn. We see the tarn through the drifts of rain which mingle with the white spray whipped up from its fermenting surface.

Without a pause we turn off and head downwards to Langdale. Suddenly we are out of the main blast of the storm and the contrast from noise to relative silence is uncanny. The lady member of our group is limping. We stop as she takes off her boot and wet stocking and I find her an adhesive dressing to cover the large weeping blister.

She talks about their plans for the rest of their week's holiday. Tomorrow should be Helvellyn, but I suggest she rests her sore heel and they dry out their gear. We discuss easy alternatives. A leisurely walk round Grasmere and Rydal lakes if it is good walking weather again, and we discuss the merits of museums and stately homes if it is not. The man smiles and says that I am encouraging laziness. Ron, a keen Lancastrian, winks at me and points out that he has discovered that the couple come from Yorkshire and a bit of culture would do them a world of good, Yorkshire being a wilderness.

We carry on and the rain is still hurling down at us, sometimes vertically, sometimes as we get farther away from the shelter of the ridge behind, horizontally. As we reach the road the wind is pushing at us again and the rain stingling like needles at our faces if we look into it. The road always seems long and it seems too long before we are splashing through the puddles back into the car park. We slip off rucksacks and the couple ask us if we will accept their Yorkshire hospitality, and join them for a 'mash o' tea'.

The café is full of steaming humanity and wet waterproofs. I recognise the elderly walker.

'Was your dog back at the car?'

He beams at me. It was indeed. Thanks. He could have shot it. He had been worried sick.

'Dogs aren't daft, I reckon,' he said. 'Nobody but a blockhead would be out on the tops on a day like this.'

No one disagreed.

Drystone Walls

The drystone walls are an important feature of the Lake District landscape. Most of them were built during the eighteenth and nineteenth centuries. There are hundreds of miles of them, stretching sometimes unbroken in straight lines right over fells and crags.

Sometimes they spread over the hillsides like nets. Some of them are boundaries, some control the grazing system, separating intake pasture from the open fell, or enclosing the better quality inby land. Sometimes funnel-shaped enclosing walls were constructed to make the gathering of sheep from the open fell simpler. The enormous amount of human effort put into their building and the endurance of the men who built them on the windswept heights strains the imagination. Nothing much is known of the builders, though accounts show that in 1794 they were paid around two shillings a day – and the day would be from dawn to sunset no doubt. Often they were paid by volume of work. In the later nineteenth century this worked out at about a shilling a yard, but this probably included collecting the stone, and certainly the digging out for the foundation. The stone was won from the fellsides themselves. The little quarries and broken outcrops where they got the stone can be seen everywhere, and stone was sledged to the site. The men must have often lived on the job, getting what shelter they could at night from the wall they built. Sometimes food was provided for the workmen, in which case their payment was reduced accordingly. Otherwise wives or children would bring their food to them.

Repairing a wall, or building a new one, is a fascinating work of art. It is a heavy three-dimensional jigsaw puzzle, and locking it together is a therapeutic exercise for anyone who thinks himself overburdened with worldly cares.

The foundations are the hardest work. First a line is laid out and the grass sods removed to the required width and the soil dug to about six inches, or less if the ground is firm. Then you collect good heavy stones and fit them into the ground. The building then commences. A drystone wall is really two walls, for you lay lines of stones on either side and fill between them with small stone fragments, the 'heartings' or fillings. Each layer of stones is placed so that the joints of those set below are covered. The walls have the heavier stones near the foot, and at certain levels are laid the 'throughs', large stones which go right through both sides of the wall and lock them together. The walls narrow towards the top, which is finished with 'cams', stones laid on their edges and all leaning in one direction. The cams seal off and secure the top and deter acrobatic sheep. Sometimes the waller will alternate cam stone sizes to produce a castellated effect. That is the theory of it and drystone walling is very simple, but many times on my walks about the district I admire a craftsman's work. There is a wall in the Duddon valley so perfectly made that I have to stop and enjoy the sight of it. What a man was this who could create such a thing of beauty from crude untooled rock! The stones are set absolutely flush, the line and the tapering is perfect. I get more enjoyment out of seeing that wall than I would get from seeing a great master's work in an art gallery.

Not far from Ulpha also in the Duddon valley is a wall that is mind-boggling. At first glance it is a normal wall which you might pass by, noticing vaguely that some of the stones are large. Stop and look again, and you see that they are quite enormous and if you have ever built a wall, placing each stone, turning each this way and that until it fits just right, then you can only be staggered at the thought of someone lifting such stones as these, let alone moving them about and fitting them flush and safe. Many of them weigh several hundredweights. I have this mental image of two brothers back in the early nineteenth century. Tom, the brainy one, and this huge monster of a man, like Hugh Hird of Troubeck, who is said to have lifted the great beam of Kentmere Hall into position after ten men had failed to move it. I can imagine Tom saying to him, 'Get that big round stone over and put it here,' and the huge man lumbering over to it, his great thick arms dangling loosely from his massive shoulders.

'This one, Tom?' he roars.

'That's it.'

The legs, like tree trunks, bend, the great hands grip, and he is holding the stone up, leaning back slightly as he ambles forward.

'Where do you want it, Tom?'

'Right there. No, the other way up. Turn it round. Yes that'll do.' Crash!

Maybe it was not like that. Maybe two strong men worked in unison, but that is hard to believe because unison is hard to achieve and it is dangerous to fingers and toes when movement is uncoordinated. Some of us have scars to prove it.

It was George, our driver who showed me how to wall. He always pleaded he was no expert, but, like all craftsmen, he made it look so simple. Having picked up a stone he would never put it down, he would find a place where it would fit somewhere. And, like the best wallers I have watched, he would not place the stone in position but offer it towards its chosen place and drop it there, or throw it. The solidity of the 'clunk' as it landed told him that it fitted and should stay there. If it was not quite right the sound would be different and the stone would rock, in which case he would pick it up and turn it round or drop it in somewhere else, then reach for the next stone. He could also build the back wall as smoothly and as solidly as the side he was working from. I have to keep climbing over to make sure I have it right.

What is fascinating is the variety and shapes of the rocks you are working with. The most satisfying areas to work in are those which give you a good mixture of flat stones, blocks, and 'beck-bottom' sphericals. If you wish to know the local geology of the Lake District you have only to look at the nearest drystone wall and it is all there, for none of the stone has been carried far. In one wall I built the bulk of the material is sedimentary, Silurian rock, of various densities, but mixed in is a surprising variety of Borrowdale volcanics, left by the ice melt after the last glaciation.

Walling is really a job for a 'loner', one who can tolerate his own company. I daresay it is possible but I have never seen two wallers working well together. Each man has his own style of work and it rarely matches his mate's. Far better to work on separate stints. It is possible to see on some of the old wall lengths where the builders have changed. Given the general principle of wall building, the actual working methods vary with the type of material to hand. Building with the small rough stones of limestone is more difficult than with Silurian slabs.

Once you get into building a wall, it becomes all-absorbing and you might forget the passage of time. We tried the experiment of organising a course in walling and inviting the general public. All sorts of people turned up. Among them was an elegant lady in a white safari outfit with peep-toe sandals. She explained in a highly cultured voice that she had not come to try her hand but to watch. I smiled to myself because I knew what would happen. It was not long before I heard her say, 'I think this rock will fit there.' She was offering a thin slab to the volunteer worker with her white-gloved hand. Two hours later she was thoroughly enjoying herself at a section of wall and her safari outfit was somewhat khaki down the front. I feared for her toes but she finished unscathed. Among the volunteers were two keen professional wallers. One had come from across the border to see how the English walls were built. Another came from Northumberland as he wanted to try his hand with stone other than his local sandstones and limestones. A lady from the local radio station, who had come to record visitors' reaction to the scheme, could be seen later building away with the rest, her recording machine put aside.

Just before lunch the farmer whose wall we were working on came to see how far we had got and his mouth dropped open in amazement as he saw the crowd working. There were elderly people and teenagers. Whole family groups and loners. People of all kinds. The instructors were having to run about giving advice here, helping to put a 'through' in there. There was a Dutch couple. He explained in faltering English that they had no walls where they came from, but on their holiday here the walls were the first thing they noticed and they wanted to see how we made them stand without mortar. At the end of the day the man said,

166

'We try again on our holiday next year.' There was also a retired Australian sheep farmer amongst us. 'Getting involved personally,' he explained, heightened the enjoyment. He was having the holiday of his lifetime.

When the last man had gone, I looked along the wall which had earlier been a ruin and an eyesore, and it looked good. It was patchy in quality to say the least, but it stood firm and it will stand firm for many years – longer than a mortared wall. For as the steep ground the walls are built on moves and settles the drystone walls – miles upon miles of them crossing and recrossing the landscape – flex with it and remain attached as if they have grown naturally.

Apparitions and Hallucinations

A small search team had been out on a night search and I was asked if I could report to Grasmere police station early the following morning for 'what could be a false alarm'. Well, one has to make sure; false alarms have proved to be positive on occasions.

The party assembled numbered twenty because it had been decided that only a token search was needed. The sergeant who was briefing us was firm in his opinion that we were just 'going for a nice fell walk'. 'You've got good weather for it,' he said, then he explained.

'Last night at about twenty hundred hours two couples from a nearby hotel were standing in the hotel grounds when, they say, they saw a flying saucer which hovered a while, then appeared to land on the fell. The position they pointed out to us was towards Easedale Tarn. Now, we don't know what they saw. I don't believe in flying saucers personally, but these were very sincere sober people. They could have seen an aircraft which possibly could have crashed. Although we've not been able to trace that there is a missing aircraft I suggest that we ought to take no chances. Last night's search party went to Easedale Tarn and saw nothing. I suggest that you too lay out a search in that general direction and I leave the organisation in your capable hands.'

There was a bit of facetiousness all round, then we laid out a rough plan. I would take eight men in the direction of Blind Tarn Moss, south of Easedale Tarn, Mike would take the rest up Far Easedale to the north, and we would all converge on the tarn for around one o'clock. As we went off for our 'nice fell walk', the sergeant called after us, 'And if you see any little green men, lads, I want all their names and addresses!'

The thin morning mist was lifting where it was touched by the sun. We split up at the top of the road. My party crossed the bridge onto a rough track, we went through some farm land and climbed onto the open fell. Why do I return to Blind Tarn Moss time and time again? There is nothing extraordinary about it at first as a piece of landscape. It is a cover scooped out by glaciation. The tarn it once held was eventually filled in with many centuries of silt and encroaching rushes. But the atmosphere on the approach is exciting to me, for the valley is filled with juniper bushes, and the unusual feature is the huge variety of bush and tree shapes. From a distance one could confuse *Juniperus communis* with gorse, but it is not spiny like gorse and has no gaudy yellow flowers. It is the only British representative of the cypress family, and has much decreased for some odd reason in many parts of our islands. Some of the bushes here grow tall like church spires, some are spherical like huge green puff-balls, some strangely bent and angled like crouching witches, some domed like umbrellas, some flat like tables. Doubtless browsing by hungry sheep on young shoots has had some effect, but the overall impression is as if a mad gardener has gone around the large area with a pair of shears devising some wild plan

169

of topiary. The juniper wood looks contrived and artificial, but it is wholly natural and I suppose that, to me, is the attraction. But is there some other attraction to me too, some strange magnetism?

Well, I like juniper. Many of the Lake District valleys have their areas of junipers and once the charcoal obtained from them was much valued by the local gunpowder mills. To the local people they must have been a valuable source of medicine. The berries contain oils; now they are largely used for flavouring gin, but they were once greatly valued for urinary complaints. The great seventeenth-century herbalist, Culpeper, had great faith in it as a magical cure-all, 'excellent against the bites of venomous beasts – no better remedy for wind in any part of the body – cough – shortness of breath – convulsions – speedy delivery to pregnant women – they strengthen the brain – the nerves – the limbs of the body. A lye made from the ashes of the wood, and the body bathed with it cures the itch, scabs, leprosy etc.' If a flying saucer had landed I am inclined to believe that they had come to collect a supply of the valuable herb! The berry takes two years to ripen. I enjoy a few green berries for their sharp clean taste. The ripe black berries are sickly-sweet.

I spread my party out in line and we walked through the junipers and over some very wet ground towards Blind Tarn. We had no idea what we were supposed to be looking for, perhaps pieces of aircraft. We had no radios so I called out, 'Spread out and continue in line to the foot of Yew Crag.' In fact we had to spread out wider than we intended when we left the junipers because we were soon over our boot tops in water. I found myself on a quaking bog, a large area of moss and rushes thick enough to hold my weight, but floating and rippling sluggishly as I distributed it. I detoured round it to the north and eventually found myself, with two other searchers, under Yew Crag and standing on

170

what was obviously at one time the west of the now silted-up tarn.

And here I can only report what we saw. In the centre of the very large rush bed that had been the tarn was a quite distinct completely circular area of flattened rush. It was I suppose some fifty feet or more in diameter. We stood there and looked at it and laughed. There was no explanation we could readily think of. I suggested a whirlwind. Then Ken, one of the searchers, brought our attention to the smell. We noticed it then too. It was a distinct smell of ozone. This clinched it for another member of our party who said that there had obviously been an electrical storm and lightning had struck there, and what the observers had seen was in fact a fireball or a thunderbolt. The others arrived and agreed it was peculiar. One suggestion was that it resembled the flattened area produced by a helicopter and maybe what had been seen was a night-flying chopper?

Well there was no sign of pieces of wreckage so we searched on over the hill towards Easedale Tarn. But as we rested and looked back from the higher position, we saw the circular area quite distinctly. We opened our pack lunches and flasks and speculated. Pete put an interesting point.

'If I saw a flying saucer I'd keep it to myself. If I started putting it about everyone would think I was daft. So, I ask myself, how many people have seen UFOs and said nowt for the same reason?'

Then we went on to talk about hallucinations. Tom said that as he was walking alone down from Greenup Edge one late afternoon he saw a man coming up the winding path towards him leading a horse. Both man and animal were only in view from time to time as they walked round rock step obstructions, or appeared from behind obscuring ground. But although Tom expected to meet them he never did. He assumed that somehow they had climbed past him

171

on another path, but when he reached the point where he had last seen them, there were human footprints in the soft ground in quantity, but none at all of a horse. He looked back for a long time at the skyline expecting the pair to appear, but they never did. He looked for hoof prints all the way down the valley without success. He had reckoned then he had seen a ghost.

We agreed that the effect of distance, sometimes of light or moving mist, or heat waves produce odd effects – hallucinations are not uncommon on the fells. A distant shape, which you might assume is a bush, moves if you stare at it for a while. You are then convinced that it is a person. On a mountain search there are frequent false alarms. Rocks against the skyline often appear to move, and they could hide an army anyway. One odd group of such rocks on Ullock Pike, Skiddaw, is known as 'Watches'. Border raiders in the old days could well have mistaken the group as human guards, and they must have avoided the craggy hills because of the dangerous possibilities of surprise. I pointed out the odd shapes of the junipers below us; in some lights they might look like an army. They too could certainly hide one.

I reminded the team about the classic hallucination, if that is what it was. It is a fascinating story and is documented. It goes back to Midsummer Eve, 1735, when a farm labourer was walking by Souther Fell. There is nothing extraordinary about the shape of Souther Fell. Its unusual feature is that it stands inside a great natural mote; a river which rejoices in the grand Celtic name of Glenderamackin curls almost completely round the fell, a diameter of about five miles. Souther is a spur of the fell of Blencathra and rises only to 1680 feet. It presents an unexciting face eastwards, and its crags are on the north. It is not on any route from anywhere to anywhere, so the labourer, looking up at the fell, was naturally surprised to see a whole army on the march along the eastern flank. They appeared to come in separate groups from the northern end, finishing their manoeuvres outwards and then upwards again to the hummocks at the sourthern end. When he told his story he was ridiculed by everyone. But on Midsummer Eve two years later, a Mr Lancaster, the employer of the farm labourer, happened to look up at the fell and was surprised to see horses with some men following them. However he did not take too much account of this, but when he looked up again later he saw that the men had mounted their horses and, as he stared up the fell at them into that long-shadowed light before twilight, he rubbed his eyes and saw that following the mounted men – was a great body of men, marching in order five abreast. He ran and called out his family, and they all watched the manoeuvres in detail. The officers were riding up and down the ranks keeping the lines in good order. They continued to watch as the men marched over the rim of the fell in the fading daylight. The Lancaster family too were ridiculed when they talked about the apparition and there were no further reports until eight years later – 1745, again on Midsummer Eve. The Lancasters' attention was again drawn to the fell and after watching some indistinct shapes with fearful flesh-creeping anticipation, they saw the mounted men and the army again marching over the fell. This time they called out all their neighbours. At least twenty-six people (for it was that number that testified on oath before a magistrate next day) saw the huge body of men marching – and this time with horse-drawn carts and carriages which could not have got on the fell anyway. There was apparently nothing shadowy about the vision. It was all very distinct, and the troops were strung out for over half a mile, only becoming obscured when the light began

173

to fade. The watchers were so convinced that what they had seen was real, that some of them went up to the fell on the following day to look for tracks. There were none. After this report it was inevitable that others would confess that they had seen similar apparitions at midsummer in other years on the fell and not reported it for fear of ridicule. One such was a Mr Wren who stated that he was with one of his farm labourers and they both saw a man with a dog attempting to round up some horses on the fell, but they were bolting about with such speed that they both assumed that if they searched the fell at first dawn they might find the corpses of horses, man, or dog. They did search and found nothing, not even tracks, so they kept quiet about it.

Then Jack reminded me of an incident on a course a few years ago when we were with a group of teenagers eating our lunch at Sty Head Pass in wet saturating drizzle, smothered in waterproofs. Suddenly out of the mist from the Wasdale direction appeared a man wearing a neat city suit, smart shoes, a bowler hat, and carrying a brief case. We stared at him and I remember pinching myself. He wished us good day as he walked past back into the mist in the direction of Borrowdale. He was real enough. But where he came from, dressed as he was, and where he was going will remain a mystery. Strangely we had heard stories of similar encounters. A Kendal acquaintance said that he had met the man on Fairfield summit. The brief case, he said, was stuffed with religious tracts. The man had tried to convert him. We had also had other reports that he had been seen by other people on Scafell Pike, Skiddaw, and Coniston Old Man.

Mountain conditions seem to induce hallucinations, particularly to those under stress. Nick Estcourt, climbing alone in snow at night with equipment for Camp 5 on the 1975 Everest expedition, records that he was followed by another climber whom he could not identify and who would not answer to his call. Bright moonlight, the snow reflection, and the clear air showed the figure up quite clearly and he watched its arms and legs moving as it worked out the climb below. Nick turned round several times in the climb to observe the following figure still there, but on reaching his destination he could look all the way back down to the starting point and it was no longer in sight. In fact there was not, and could not have been, anyone following him at all.

There are other famous instances. Frank Smythe on the 1933 Everest expedition was climbing alone at 27,000 feet when he became convinced for a time that he was tied to a second man on a rope. It was not so. And on the first ascent of the Matterhorn in 1865, after three of his companions and a guide had fallen to their death, Whymper records that as he was descending with his two remaining guides they saw 'a mighty arch' rise upwards before them through the clouds and into the sky. It was colourless, he records, and noiseless. Then as they watched in amazement the shape of two crosses developed, one on either side.

These experiences though were at an extreme height and in stress conditions. But hallucinations, or psychic phenonema are not unknown at lower levels in the mountains. The most famous phantom in Britain is the Grey Man of Ben Macdhui in the Cairngorms, low by international standards at something over four thousand feet. There are many reports of lone walkers being followed by this giant of a phantom, his footsteps crunching in the snow behind them. The tales cannot be lightly dismissed as there have been some very reliable witnesses. One of the earliest encounters was reported by a highly renowned and accomplished pioneer of mountaineering, John Norman Collie, Professor of Organic Chemistry of University College, London. He said that when climbing Ben Macdhui in the

175

snow and mist alone, (though it was the first time he had done this) he heard very distinct and heavy footsteps behind him which stopped when he stopped, and restarted when he did. When he approached the summit cairn the heavy footsteps appeared to be getting nearer and nearer. He looked back to see a huge shape, bigger than any human, and he fled in terror down the mountain. Mountaineers could easily explain the huge shape as the trick of light on cloud producing what is known as a 'brocken spectre'. But Professor Collie, with his long mountaineering experience at home and abroad, must have been familiar enough with this phenomenon to recognise the conditions which produce it. Then there were the heavy crunching footsteps. He was so affected by the experience that, although he lived fairly near to the mountain, he never ventured onto that particular summit again.

Brocken spectres are not unusual. They are caused by sunshine filtering through the mist behind the viewer and casting the viewer's huge shadow onto a bank of mist in front. Once while on patrol on Striding Edge, Helvellyn, I and all who walked the edge observed this phenomenon for a whole hour. The cove above Red Tarn below the edge was filled with thick towering cloud and the sun threw our shadows onto it. It appeared as if each walker was accompanied by a dark giant. The walkers were fascinated by the sight and were jumping up and down and waving their arms about as if they were inebriated to produce effects.

Every mountaineering area in the world must have its share of ghost stories. All sorts of happenings must materialise in the Celtic twilight of the Welsh and Scottish hills. But there are not many reported incidents in the Lake District hills. There are stories. In the old days when roads were few and consecrated burial grounds were very far between, the coffins with the dead were carried for miles over the rough fell footpaths, followed by the mourners. Many of these old by-ways are still called by the locals 'corpse roads'. Burnmoor, between Eskdale and Wasdale, is reputed to be haunted by a horse carrying a coffin. In the last century a funeral cortege was travelling over the high track, with a coffin with the corpse of a young boy, fastened to the back of a pony. At one point, it is said, something in the gathering murk of the summit made the pony take fright and it bolted. Although the mourners searched they could find no trace of the pony or its load which had completely vanished in the mist. Not long afterwards the mother of the boy, never really recovering from her shock at the disappearance of her son's body, died too. Another cortege followed the same route. This time the second pony shied at the same spot in the mist and made off. An extensive search was made and the searchers eventually found – not the pony carrying the dead woman, but the first pony with the boy's body. The second pony was never found and it was at last assumed to have been swallowed up in the deep bogs below Scafell's flank. It is said that travellers over Burnmoor in the mist sometimes see the dark shape of a pony carrying a coffin.

The shape of mountains and crags themselves can play tricks too. In boyhood William Wordsworth, while rowing on a lake in the twilight, was terrified by the sight of a great crag which seemed to be moving towards him. He had borrowed, without permission, a boat moored at Patterdale and he rowed out into Ullswater. He describes the experience in *The Prelude:*

'... from behind that craggy steep till then
The Horizon's bound, a huge peak, black and huge,
As if with voluntary power instinct
Upreared its head. I struck and struck again

177

And growing still in stature the grim shape
Towered up between me and the stars, and still
For so it seemed, with no purpose of its own
And measured motion like a living thing,
Strode after me…'

He was terrified by the experience which affected him for
some time –

'… no familiar shapes
Remained, no pleasant images of trees,
Of sea or sky, no colours of green fields,
But huge and mighty forms, that do not live
Like living men, moved slowly through the mind
By day, and were a trouble to my dreams.'

Probably the best-known phantom in the Lake District
however is the Crier of Claife. Claife Heights is no mountain. It is a very steep and beautiful wooded ridge on the
west side of Windermere, north of the ferry, with public
footpaths through it enjoyed by hundreds of walkers every
year. For many generations it has been considered to be
haunted and some local people in the parish still take it
fairly seriously. The beginning is probably half-truth or
legend. It used to be the custom for travellers to call for the
ferryman if he did not happen to be on the right side of the
lake. One night the ferryman, while enjoying a drink with
friends at the Ferry Inn, was called from the other side of
the lake by what was described as a 'weird' cry. He took the
ferry across and did not return. A search was made for him
and he was eventually found wandering after apparently
losing his mind. It is said that after this time the cry was
heard on many occasions, and men (apparently never
women) were lured by the cry and did not return. Eventual-

ly it was arranged for a priest to exorcise the ghost and this he did, banishing the Spirit to a quarried hollow on the heights, to stay there until 'it was possible for men to cross Windermere on foot'. Still legend? The hollow is known to the local people and is in fact marked on the 1:25000 Ordnance Survey maps for all to see (Ref. 384982). The exorcism seemed to have been only partly effective. It is anyway, from time to time, possible to cross Windermere on foot. I did it during the great freeze-up of 1964. (In fact at that time motorists drove for considerable distances on the ice.) Several local people who happen to be my neighbours believe that the phantom still walks, and those who have met the apparition are not inclined to talk about it for fear of ridicule. A friend of mine, who is scrupulously honest and down to earth, talked about his experience after a good meal and a drink or two in congenial company, and he told me this tale, his wife sitting next to him with her face tense and white.

'You know what it was like after the war. We were just married and we were broke. So now and then I used to do a bit o' poaching to help make ends meet. An odd rabbit or a pheasant helped out a bit. Well, one nice evening, with promise of a good moonlight later, I decided to go up onto Claife, and because the weather was so good the wife thought she might like to come with me. So we went up from Far Sawrey onto the ridge paths and when we had gone some distance without any luck we heard somebody coming up behind us. We looked back and there was this chap coming up in t' gloom and he was, we thought, wearing a duffle jacket. You know those big woollen coats with a hood. You could get them from government surplus stores at the time quite cheap. As we stopped and looked back he stopped too. As we walked on he followed. We kept on a bit like this, both of us stopping and starting and him getting a bit closer, so I hid the shotgun in t' bracken thinking he might be a gamekeeper. I looked back and he had his hood up and I couldn't see his face. Well, as he seemed bent on catching us up we moved on quickly and pretty soon we were running. I looked back after a while and he was still coming fast as we were. I could hear him panting. Well after a bit the wife was all in and she said, "That's it. I can't run any more." So I thought, "Boogar this, I'll face the man. Perhaps he's mad." Well I heard him coming up the hill towards us and he sounded absolutely whacked. His breath was coming in and out like bellows and he was wheezing away like a steam engine – a sort of hollow wheeze.' (Here he imitated the noise.)

'Well, I stood there and stopped and him still wheezing away, and we faced each other. I still couldn't see his face. I didn't think he was a local man. I thought he was some sort of nut. Well, we kept on standing there, him still wheezing, and I said to t' wife, "Come on. The man's a fool. We're going home," and we walked on and took another way home. I looked back once or twice but the man seemed to have given up.

'Well, we thought no more of this for – oh, I suppose it would be two or three years or more. And I never remembered this bloke except as a mysterious nutter. Then one night the wife and me were sitting in the local when talk got around to the Crier of Claife and we were having a laugh about it. But there was an old chap there whom we knew, and he wasn't laughing. Then he said, "I saw it y' know. The Crier –" Then he said, "That's not really true. I didn't actually see it, but I heard it." I asked him what it sounded like. "Well," he said, "it was like very heavy breathing. Like this –" and he imitated the noise. "They say it's the ghost of a monk." Then – good God! – it hit us all of a sudden. The noise, the duffle coat – well, you don't often see a monk's habit – the breathing. The wife nearly passed out.'

I cannot say that in all the mileage I have done on the fells I have ever had an hallucination. But I do know that it is sometimes hardly possible to separate reality from imagination. Such is the roughness of the ground, with undulations, hollows, holes, and blocks of rock and jutting crags, that it is possible to see people at one moment and completely lose them the next.

Then there are the odd coincidences. I was walking over a snow covered pathless moor one day. The weather was clear and I could see for a very great distance. For absolutely no reason at all the name of a casual acquaintance came to my mind as I walked. Then some time later I saw a moving speck in the distance as a walker approached over the pathless waste. There was not another person in sight. As we walked closer to each other we moved so that we would meet to pass the time of day. When we did meet I saw to my astonishment that it was Peter, the man who had come into my mind earlier.

Then there is the surprising degree of heightened awareness at moments on the mountain. I was climbing Broad Stand, a rock problem between Scafell Pike and Scafell which is one of those moves you can accomplish with ease so long as you bring your foot up about ear-height without losing your balance. As I pulled myself upright to the path above there was a man waiting to come down. We exchanged only a split-second greeting and parted. Two or three years later I was in Patterdale Youth Hostel and was aware that a man was staring at me.

'Sorry,' he said, 'but I think we've met and I can't remember where.'

'Yes,' I said, 'We passed each other on Broad Strand some years ago.'

'That's right!' he exclaimed, and we both laughed in amazement that we could possibly have both remembered the split-second encounter.

There is another peculiar experience that I have had on a small number of occasions when I have been pushing myself somewhat on the fell. I once had a strenuous day in the snow, instructing on a course, when I was called out with a rescue team to investigate some cries of help on Pavey Ark, in the Langdale Pikes. We went back up the fell and at the far end of Stickle Tarn below the great crag of Pavey the snow was soft and deep and it was an effort pushing in my feet and heaving them out again. We were told then that some teenagers were crag-fast in Easy Gully. On the long approach my legs were moving automatically up and down and I was taking in breath rhythmically. My body felt numb and it seemed to be operating with no conscious effort – as if it was working on automatic pilot. Then I had the feeling that I was up ahead and climbing the gully while in fact my body was still moving automatically down below. I could see myself! After what must have only been a second or so of this odd experience I became frightened and made what I supposed to be a conscious successful effort to reunite my real self with my body. Is this hallucination?

Well, we met at Easedale Tarn to end the search, without seeing the flying saucer. But as Pete said as we sat and watched a group of walkers staggering towards us dressed as if they were going to a vicarage tea party, 'You see some weird things on t' fell. A saucer or two would be neither here nor there.'

Litter

The most depressing and demoralising sight that can face any manager of a public open space is a deserted picnic area after the crowds have gone. I am quite sure that the British must be amongst the untidiest nations in the world. They are sneaky too. Litter is not thrown down as a gesture of defiance to authority. It is surreptitiously dropped or let slide, or is merely left when the culprit walks away. It is a sin which is not confined to one level of society. The wealthy leave expensive rubbish, the poor leave common rubbish. Nor is it anything to do with the standard of education. One of the most blatant offences, the throwing of litter into a beautiful tarn, was perpetrated by a university lecturer who tried to cover the shame of being caught by trying to start a contentious and devious discussion on what was and was not litter. Nor has it much to do with race; the Celtic British are just as piggy as the Anglo-Saxons and the immigrants soon catch the disease. Nor are visitors more untidy than locals. For sheer volume of litter the locals win hands down.

I was once asked to speak at a village Women's Institute. By chance I was going through the village a week or so before I was due to speak and I stopped and had a walk around. At one point the beck, which ran through the village, went through a wooded hollow. The wood was only sketchily fenced and a road ran along the top of it. Here was an ideal village dumping ground I thought, and I was right. There was an appalling mess only half-hidden in the undergrowth. I made a list of all the items in the beck and the bushes around, including perambulators, bicycle wheels and frames, refrigerators, an old television set, an assortment of mattresses, bundles of magazines, rags, and sacks of bottles. When I gave my talk I mentioned litter. I put the popular local view that tourists brought their rubbish and there were nods of agreement. I said then that not far from a 'certain village' a lot of rubbish had been dumped in a beck and perhaps the tourists brought that too? I then proceeded to read out the list. There were one or two red faces. A few weeks after the talk I went back and was happy to see that the rubbish dump had been miraculously spirited away.

Quick 'solutions' to the 'litter problem' are readily volunteered. Everyone is an expert. All the practical suggestions have been tried, failed, or found wanting. Typically, a letter to a local paper complained about the mess and the overflowing litter bins at a picnic site (not, I hasten to add under the management of the National Park) and the writer said that she had recently spent some time at a royal park open to the public where there were no trash bins or unsightly notices, but everyone took their litter home, or put it in bags provided at certain points. She suggested that this was the answer – 'treat people with respect and they will show respect.' I wrote to the agent for that royal park and asked if the writer had got the facts right. The reply was rapid and to the point. He was very happy to hear someone praising his park for its cleanliness, but no, a considerable amount of man hours was spent in picking up litter and the sack system was not an answer. If the place looked clean it was because estate workers were beavering away keeping it so. The mess some people left was terrible, and if I had any suggestions on how to control the situation efficiently he would be grateful.

I have been to quite a few conferences to discuss the litter problem. I go to them hopefully to pick up ideas. To hear new suggestions on how the public can be rapidly educated to throw off the habits of generations. I usually come away saddened, sometimes angered. I have heard planners, who have never stopped to examine litter let alone pick it up, suggesting how proper site design can discourage littering. I have heard a sociologist speak at length on why people drop litter. He appeared to think that litter was only paper bags and orange peel, and was completely unaware that the main problem was drink cans, non-returnable bottles, cartons and wrappers by the ton, not to mention some unsavoury items that revolt the stomach. I have heard local politicians make some clever remarks and jokes about the litter problem. The same ones. (Perhaps there is a local politicians' joke book?) They do not help. Time and again I have heard agents, site managers, site wardens say that they have solved their litter problem by a clever or cunning stratagem, and they really believe it. Investigation showed that all deceived themselves. One manager, making this statement on site to a party of us on a course, claimed that his carefully worded signs had solved his problem, and while he was speaking one of us was kicking drink cans by the dozen out of their hiding place in the nearby bushes. He continued to talk without batting an eyelid. I heard a manager say at a conference that his authority had solved the litter problem by taking the receptacles away. I have heard this a thousand times. As it happened I had visited his site only the previous day and it was filthy with litter that had been lying in the bracken for months. There are none so blind as those who do not take the trouble to see. I heard another manager telling a party of visiting foreign national park managers and rangers that he had no litter problem, the public respected his small informal picnic areas. I had to bite my tongue. My own men cleaned up his picnic areas weekly as they passed.

The suggestions from the conferences on litter are tiresomely repetitive. One – more litter receptacles. That means more emptying services which is fine if you can pay for it, and it also means that receptacles have to be well designed to fit their place, otherwise they become litter themselves. Two – less receptacles. That depends upon the site. In remote areas the absence of receptacles is right. On heavily used sites you cannot get away with it. Three – no receptacles at all and 'Take your litter home' signs. You can fool yourselves that this really works too if you drive quickly by and do not stop to look behind walls and bushes. Four – heavier fines for offenders and on-the-spot fines. But how do you catch offenders? Most are not litter throwers, but crafty litter leavers. In the end you have to get down to cleaning up; all the talk in the world about the problem will do no good. I once went to a village parish council meeting where there was a long discussion about the rubbish problem on the village green. I stood as much as I could and then suggested that if we all got off our butt-ends we could solve the problem of the rubbish around the village green in one hour. We did it in less.

In the end, if you have any pride in the area at all, you have to arrange for scavenging. Clearing up the mess after the crowds have gone is a nasty and expensive business, but woe betide the managers of an area who do not tidy up regularly, for litter breeds litter. Long experience has taught me that whereas a place which starts spotlessly clean remains unlittered for a reasonably long period (at least many people seem to have a conscience about being the first to desecrate a tidy area), uncleared litter breeds litter fast. I have eight handymen working with four vehicles all the season. They clean up all the areas outside the main villages where motorists picnic. If anyone wants views on the litter problem let him ask one of them. Every year hundreds of volunteers, groups of adults and schoolchildren, and individuals, clean up the fells and the public paths and the shallows of the lakes. They do a fantastic job. When someone looks around, smiles at me and says, 'How lucky you are! You don't appear to have a litter problem here,' I find it extremely difficult to think of a suitable reply.

When people see other people clearing litter – particularly young volunteers – they almost invariably comment, 'Isn't it awful!' So, of course, none of them drops litter. If everyone seems to agree that the habit is terrible, then who drops it? The excuses given when people are caught littering are extraordinary. The most usual is, 'I'm sorry. I don't normally do that sort of thing. I can't think why I did it!' or the blatant, 'I've dropped it by accident, sorry,' or even, 'I've just put it down temporarily.' The excuses are often followed up with comments of appreciation on 'What a fine job you are doing!'

We once found an envelope on a lake-shore parking space containing some ham fat which had been presumably trimmed off someone's picnic sandwich. The envelope was addressed – so I sent one of my standard letters with particulars of the offence and time and place, giving a time limit for explanations and apologies, which, if not met satisfactorily, might be followed by legal proceedings. I received a long letter in which I was told that the owner of the envelope had not been near the lake in question in her

187

visit and that she was puzzled by the affair. She could only assume that someone else in the guest house where she was staying had picked up one of her discarded envelopes. She then went on for four pages about what a beautiful National Park we had, and how well we did in looking after it, and her personal views on the best areas and how she always did her bit for conservation. She kindly wished us well in the future. Then below her signature there was a postscript. 'I would point out that there was no litter basket in your lake-side parking spot.'

One of my driver-handymen, an ex-army major, gave what is probably the most outrageous, but what might possibly be the most astute, explanation of why people drop litter. He is a keen naturalist. He said that seventy-five per cent of litter droppers were men. In dropping his litter a man's motives were purely instinctive. He was marking his territory, in a similar way to a dog cocking its leg. When he put down his beer can he was, without knowing it, subconsciously saying, 'This is my marker. This is my land. Dispute it who dare.'

'It's basic animal instincts we're dealing with,' my friend suggested. 'Somehow the propagandists must bear that in mind.'

George was my first driver-handyman when I successfully launched the 'little and often' litter clearance years ago. There were only one or two people who responded to the newspaper ad for a driver. George was a retired southern Lake District farmer, a native, who had kept and hired horses and was a keen huntsman. When I called to interview him he did not seem to care very much about whether he got the job or not.

'I don't have to work. I've saved enough to get by. All I'm thinking about is getting out from under t' wife's feet.'

He seemed the most suitable candidate and I offered him the job on a trial basis. I went on a trip with him in the van and showed him what we were up against. He was appalled. He admitted that he had been vaguely disturbed when he saw litter at beauty spots, but he had no idea that it had reached such proportions. Like many hill farmers, (he had been a tolerable Cumberland and Westmorland style wrestler in his time too) he found the impossible challenge irresistible. He would try it. I had located all the problem areas by road-sides and I worked out a route system in which the worst litter black spots had regular visits. The mileage on some days was around a hundred miles. George did not mind, he assured me; he could see places he had never been to, and renew acquaintance with others. Between the north and south halves of the National Park is Dunmail Raise, the highest point in the main road link. It is the old boundary between England and Scotland, and in the last ten centuries the boundary between the old counties of Westmorland and Cumberland, murdered in the local government reorganisation of 1974. There is an old saying which may have had ancient and sinister origins: 'Nowt good comes o'er t' Raise.' George looked forward to going into 'enemy territory'.

It was remarkable what one dedicated man with one vehicle could do with regular visits to blackspots. His philosophy was 'get stuck in' and it was a terrible job to keep him from working a seven-day week. He would be away at dawn on some off-duty days to do a clean-up. He did the work cheerfully for the most part, singing away with his deep bass voice, but unfortunately he did not mince his words on the matter of litter dropping and there were complaints about his rudeness. He told me that one lady had said that he was 'uncouth'. I asked him what he had replied.

'Well,' he said, 'I told her that I'd been married thirty years and me wife thinks I'm couth.'

He had an uncertain temper too, though he would readily confess his sins at our briefing sessions. Whenever he began his conversation with 'I had an encounter the other day...' my heart sank. Somehow he managed to avoid being charged with threatening behaviour or assault.

'I had an encounter,' he said one day, but he smiled slyly. 'But I remember what you said about keeping my temper.'

'Tell me about it,' I groaned.

'There was this school party by their coach and they were dropping rubbish all over the place. I told t' teacher to get 'em to pick it up and he give me some lip.'

'What did you do?'

'I remembered what you'd said, though I was sore tempted to kick 'im in t' arse. I did nowt.' George paused and prolonged my agony while he lit a cigarette. 'But when I walked by him I accidentally trod on 'is toes.'

I gasped. George was no light-weight and he always wore heavy hob-nailed shepherd's boots.

'What footwear had he on, George?'

'Sandals.'

I groaned. 'What did he do?'

'Nowt. He didn't say owt either.' George gave an evil grin and looked at me sideways. 'By, by gow, his eyes watered!'

He had, of course, the Cumbrian's gift of dry ironic humour and a cunning wit. Hawkshead is a busy village. It is pretty, with timber-framed buildings overlooking narrow streets and squares and yards. William Wordsworth lodged here with local worthy, Anne Tyson, when he attended the village grammar school. That is enough to bring the tourists in by the hundreds. One day we were having a briefing session in Hawkshead's car park and a motorist came across

190

and asked George what there was in Hawkshead.

'What do you mean?' asked George politely.

'Well, there's a lot of cars in the car park and a lot of folk about. There must be some attraction here.'

George looked puzzled for a brief second, then said, 'Well –' He beckoned the man closer with a wicked look in his eye and he looked dramatically to left and right then he spoke softly. 'I'll tell thee – It's a naughty woman!'

'What?'

'Aye,' he whispered. 'Just go in t' village an' ask for Anne Tyson's cottage. Ivery one knows it!'

Then there was his inevitable answer to a motorist's question, 'Where does this road go to?'

A pause while George pushed back his cap and looked carefully at the road.

'Go to? I've known this road for sixty year' an' I've nivver seen it move anywhere.' But having availed himself of this and seen the motorist had the politeness to laugh, George then told him about the area. He was normally quite helpful.

Not so helpful though to another inquirer on almost the same spot on another day. A large car and a driver with a cultured accent.

'Does this road lead out of the valley or is it a dead end?'

''Fraid you'll have to turn back,' said George shaking his head. This, of course, was not true. He could go via Blea Tarn to Little Langdale, the next valley, but I did not feel it proper to disagree with my colleague in public. After the motorist had turned round and gone, I asked George why he had told him that.

'That man's a litter lout,' he said. 'I can tell 'em a mile off. He's not going up t' Blea Tarn road. I've just cleaned it up!'

George had many adventures, perhaps the most bizarre

191

was when he met a film company on the top of the moor on a minor road. They had permission from the Highway Authority to film, and had advised the police, but nobody had told George. In the middle of filming George drove in with his van, glaring at the men who were trying to flag him down. He surveyed all the debris and paraphernalia of filming, including masses of straw that had been spread all over the road to disguise the tarmacadam, stared with disbelief at the people parading in period costume, and bawled out in his great bass voice, 'Who's in charge here?'

The director came over in a temper which was not improved by the titters from his slaves. But he had met his match. Within minutes he was promising George solemnly that when they had finished there would be absolutely nothing to be seen.

George left them, and told me later, probably with a little disappointment, that when he returned they had in fact cleared their stuff away, though straw had been blown all over the place. All he had found was a piece of camera equipment which he had handed to the police.

George seemed inexhaustible, though I remember after a long day of cleaning up he was throwing cans from a picnic area into the back of the van and he turned to me wearily but with that wicked look still in his eye, and said, 'I wish I 'ad Mr Heinz here. I'd tell him what he could do with his fifty-seven varieties – one at a time!'

After George came the expansion of the service. He had proved that even one man could do a great deal towards keeping the area respectable. But the increase in the pressure of tourism, particularly from day visitors off the new motorway systems, meant a great increase in the volume of litter.

We have reason to be grateful for the dedication of the

(almost) retired people who have worked through the seasons on our service. They include ex-policeman, ex-servicemen, a local government officer, several ex-postmen, and young students who have acted as their mates. But all their efforts would have been of little use without the great armies of volunteers, most of them in organised groups, but many people too who have come across untidiness and have felt compelled to do their bit.

Early, in clearing the back-log of years, I also had the help of prisoners from a local prison. I am not so sure that I could accept the assurance from the governer that they were volunteers. But it was a day out for them in the open air, and I was told that as they were all serving the last month or two of their sentences they were not likely to skip. Anyway, security was not my concern; an officer would be with them and my job was to keep them busy. I must say they did some great work. As they were all in plain dungarees the public was not aware that they were prisoners, and the men had all been warned that they had not to speak to any member of the public on pain of suspension of privileges. The uniformed officer could be mistaken for an ordinary policeman. I concentrated their efforts on a large area around White Moss Common, where there were old rubbish dumps as well as visitors' litter, and on Dunmail Raise where there were years of accumulation.

On one day after I had briefed them and issued them with sacks, an open sports car driven by a pretty young lady drove slowly onto the common.

'Can any of you be so kind as to change a wheel for me?' she asked. 'I've just caught a puncture I think.'

The rush was held back by the stern prison officer.

'I'll attend to this,' he called, waving them away. 'You men carry on.'

There was a general groan and I moved them off, then

193

spread them out in a long line up the hill side. I told them to keep their neighbours in sight and pick up all that they saw, put it in the bags, and keep the line as straight as possible. We were doing fine for the first fifteen minutes or so and then, in spite of my warning, two of the men, deep in conversation with each other, drifted over the brow of the hill where I did not want them, and out of sight. I called but they did not hear me. I therefore in innocence took out my whistle (which a fell-walker is never without) and blew it. I had no idea what blind panic a whistle blast can automatically cause to an unprepared prison officer. I heard feet pounding up the road and heavy breathing behind me and the officer was there in his shirt sleeves and with filthy hands calling breathlessly, 'What happened? What happened?'

'Nothing really,' I said, beckoning down the two prisoners who had reappeared to see what all the fuss was about.

Two of the prisoners, both Londoners, were seconded to accompany me to the rubbish dumps with the collected loads. I remember our first visit to the dump.

'Cor, look at this, Frederick!' said one of them, a small bow-legged man to his colleague. He pointed to the old television sets, fridges, washing machines, cookers and scrap metal. 'There's a fortune here! I reckon we ought to move up here when we get out and start up in business!'

Frederick was suitably impressed as he inspected the dumped cars. I had a job to get them away from each visit.

A month or two later, I had gone to London for a meeting. I was walking along a platform at Euston Station when coming in the opposite direction was a smart young man in a city suit, carrying a brief case. He caught my eye, we hesitated, he grinned and touched his bowler with his rolled umbrella, and walked on. It was a few seconds later that I realised it was Frederick.

I will always remember the two very disreputable looking prisoners working alongside me and chatting away as they picked up the rubbish. One of them looked across at me.

'I was just saying, it's bloody beautiful around here. What fantastic views. First chance I get, I'm going to bring my wife to see this!'

'And I was just saying,' said his mate savagely, 'that the bastards who made this mess should have their noses rubbed in it!'

As I said, everyone has their solution to the litter problem.

Rockfall

I came upon the scene of the accident by chance. I was walking on the climber's traverse on Great Gable in a claggy mist and I saw a group of people under Napes. They were sitting round a man lying among the rock slabs. I could see that he had a climbing harness on. Sitting by him was another climber, white with shock, his hands wrapped in make-shift bandages. I looked at the man on the ground. His face was bleeding from several wounds. He was pallid.

'Anyone gone for the rescue team?' I asked.

'Yes, two people have gone down.'

'How long ago?'

'About half an hour.'

'What happened?' I asked, as I turned the casualty gently and moved an arm so that he could breathe easier.

'He was leading,' said the climber with the bandaged hands. 'I think he was hit by a falling rock. He fell about forty feet and then I held him on the rope. He fell right past me. I think it's his face mostly.'

I asked him if he was all right.

'Just slight burns to my hands.'

I knelt closer to the lying man, ran my fingers over his

196

jaw. That was all right and he was breathing easily. I ran my fingers through his hair, sticky with blood, and over his scalp. It was not possible to detect serious damage although he had not been wearing a helmet. I looked at the pupils of his eyes. They appeared normal. There was blood at one ear but I could not decide whether the bleeding was internal or was coming only from an open wound above. I saw his eyes move in my direction.

'We'll soon have you out of this,' I assured him.

I ran my fingers down his neck and higher back bone. I could feel nothing wrong. I pulled out my first-aid kit, took the loose scarf someone had put round his head and bandaged on a wound dressing. I wiped blood from around his eyes. I looked round at the audience. I picked out two young men.

'Which way were you going down?'

'Wasdale Head.'

I took out my pad, looked at my map and worked out the map reference and I wrote it down. I also wrote 'Head injuries. Possibly serious.' I gave the note to the lads and asked them to hurry safely down to Wasdale Head and telephone the police with that information. I explained that the police should have some information already, but possibly not with such detail. The police could then radio the rescue team and save time. As they ran off quickly, I called after them, 'Take care!'

I turned my attention to the patient.

'What's your name?'

'Harry.' The answer was so soft that I had to sit close. 'Sorry – to trouble you. Nuisance. What happened?'

'Your mate thinks it was a rock fall.'

'– How is he?'

'Rope burns. Otherwise all right.'

'He held me – good.'

'Yes. I'm John. Have you any pain anywhere?'

'Just my head. Not much – Have another go at walking in a bit.'

'No, Harry. We'll carry you when we get the stretcher.'

'Is it – bad, then?'

'It's a hospital repair job.'

Harry sighed. I got cotton wool and wiped away blood and saliva and adjusted the sweater pillow under his head.

'– Mother – worries sick. Had – one do in hospital. Motorbike – Bradford. But this – not – my fault was it?'

'No, Harry. It was a falling rock we reckon. You're going to have two lovely black eyes.'

'– Camping gear. Wasdale.'

'We'll fix it. Your mate will pick it up.'

'Don't worry Harry!' from his friend.

A lady came forward, and asked if a sip of brandy would help.

'No,' I said. 'Offer some to his mate though, if you like.'

I mopped his face clean again. There was little else I could do. I put some decent bandages on his mate's hands; they were raw and obviously very sore. He was still white and trembling a bit so I suggested he pulled on a spare sweater. Several people helped him with this and I asked him if he wanted to get off the hill.

'No,' I said. 'Offer some to his mate though, if you like.'
worry Harry! Stretcher team's on the way.'

A long wait. Harry could still talk. I asked him about his camp site, how long he had been there, what his plans were. He answered slowly but coherently, and I can only marvel at his acceptance of the situation. But time dragged on. He did not complain, but at one stage he said simply, 'Can't see properly – now.'

'I'm not surprised, Harry,' I answered. 'Like I said – you're getting two lovely black eyes. Your face is bruised

198

and swollen. We really need a couple of raw steaks but no one seems to have any around here.'

Then as time dragged on, and on and on, I began to worry. His speech became more of an effort. I did my sums. Say one hour to get down and raise the alarm. Twenty minutes perhaps for the pack-man to set off from the valley. Another hour for him to reach me? I looked at my watch. Two and a half hours gone. Surely any time now. Which team? It could be Keswick or Wasdale. I broke open some Kendal mintcake and offered some to Harry's mate and ate some myself. Harry's mate was now also suffering strain. He came over and whispered in my ear, 'Is he going to be all right?'

'Yes,' I answered.

'Straight?'

'I'm no expert. I think so. With luck the team doctor will be up soon.'

In the event it was George, sweating under the weight of the first-aid pack. I moved down to meet him and walked back up with him and explained.

'Facial. Probably head injuries too. I can't find anything else.' I left it at that. George is the expert first-aider. I could confidently leave everything to him. There were other Keswick team members sweating up behind, appearing one by one out of the mist. And the stretcher. With the fell walkers standing around too who could be brought in to help with the carry if need be, I felt it was time to bow out. They would head for Borrowdale. I was bound for Wasdale Head.

Harry's mate refused to go down with me. 'No. I'll go down with Harry. To the hospital. Somebody'll give us a lift back to Wasdale for the gear.'

He accepted my offer to carry his climbing gear down. I would leave it at the hotel. I moved over to Harry to say my farewell. I knelt by him.

'You're all right now. This is the Keswick team. They'll have you down in no time.'

He turned his head slightly my way as George replaced my wound pad with a fresh one.

'– Sorry – to have been – trouble.'

'No trouble. Cheers lad!'

I felt I needed to say more, but what else could I say? I felt guilty even about going down to Wasdale Head, but I had done my whack. He was in expert hands. I told myself that he would be all right. I washed my hands in the beck, and picked my way below the mist into the dazzling green of the lower valley.

I heard afterwards that he died in hospital after two days. The shock was terrible. I had sat with him for so long. I had known him. I feel very little about carrying a dead body off the fell, because I never knew the occupier of the body. The person does not exist and to me he never existed. But for a time, God knows for a long time, I knew Harry.

———————————————

Spring Holiday

A friend who saw me taking colour photographs asked whether I preferred spring or autumn. I was hard put to admit a preference. For dramatic and exciting colour give me the hot embers of autumn! Autumn assaults the senses. It shouts. But can a camera lens do justice to the cool subtle colours of new-kindled spring? Spring seduces. It whispers.

'Spring's too green,' suggested my friend.

Too green? How unobservant and insensitive! Yes, there is green. But what is green? There is no standard 'leaf green' like the one labelled in my watercolour paint box I had as a child. I found that I could make a thousand greens by mixing blues and yellows; they are all there and more when I look at the sunlit woods across the bright green pasture of new grass. There are greens from bright yellow to blue, but there are also reds and purples of unopened leaf buds. Through the tree gaps beyond the green haze of bursting buds, last year's bracken still burns dusky brown; the trunks and limbs of trees still show their beauty – silver, white, and red of birches, yellow-grey of ashes, green moss and lichen covered oaks.

If the appearance of the distant woods in early May is

pleasing, how much more the close encounter. I dawdle along the lane towards the wood and from the hedges the pure white blossom of blackthorn splashes across my vision like breakers of frozen sea foam. The large gean, the wild cherry, is lit with pink flower buds. The milk-white light of full-opened blossom is already showering petals like snow, and the new-spring leaves are red. These are the curtain openers as the stage chorus breaks into song: blackbird and songthrush, great tit and chaffinch, the yaffle of a wood-pecker, mew of buzzard, the rapid gossip of the newly arrived swallow.

On the bank which supports the hedge there are prim-roses and lesser celandine, the yellow glory of the first dandelions, the prodigious gold of the gorse bushes. The white fairy-gold of the impatient coltsfoot which could not wait for spring has been with us for weeks.

Across the field on the knoll is the single ash. It has shown the beauty of its bare limbs against the sky all winter, each branch rising from the trunk then curving out and down, and its newer twigs rising upwards again at the tips. It is not a shape so much as an elegant gesture. I have admired it so long that I was unprepared for change. But change it has. The winter shape is now punctuated with black bursting buds and purple flowers. It is still beautiful yet it is disturbing. It is like suddenly realising that the girl you have distantly admired is pregnant.

Crossing the field to the wood I admire the budding oaks. It is difficult to describe their colour. In the mass they vary between dusky pink and tawny and gold, depending on their time. After oaks the birches dominate the chorus of colour and they vary too, the laggards still glow with purple buds and the rest show masses of tiny leaves like green smoke. The hawthorn trees, remnants of what was a hedge by the wood, vary for some are wide open and bright green

202

and others show red shoots and leaves. Beech in full leaf now glow as if from some bright inner light. Alder buds still show purple and the dying catkins hang brown. The goat willows are opening grey, and their catkins are now grey-green. The hazel undercover varies from yellow-brown of the leaflets and twigs to red. Here and there dark, almost blue, areas show the stands of evergreens, yew and Scots pine.

Below the cloud of subtle colours the bracken in the glades in some lights is almost pink. And all this mass of colour of tree cover and floor is changing daily as new leaf time advances. It changes too from minute to minute in the soft changing light and cloud shadows that belong to early May.

I step into the wood and the miracle of the flowers of early spring are everywhere. There are still drifts and splashes of daffodils, not the showy King Alfreds of the garden, but the little woodland blooms, milk-white and lemon. Everywhere under the trees there is wood sorrel with clean new shamrock-like leaves which I (and country children) like to chew to quench the thirst. Now they show their delicate pink flowers everywhere. Dogs mercury – now that is a green carpet and the flowers are green, but watch how the wind moves among it to make patterns of varying shades. Then everywhere in the moist areas the shining white stars of wood anemone, and in the wetness the glowing gold of marsh marigold. But in looking for flowers one must take care not to miss the intimate beauty of the new bright cushions of moss, the new-varnished leaves of cuckoo pint, the arum lily, and the aromatic smell of new mint and wild garlic.

On the fell the bracken shows no sign of green, but here and there the first shoots are coming up coiled like clock springs. To walk the fell in spring sunshine is a delight. At long last the warm outer garments can be discarded – but carried still because winter has not quit the scene; it has merely retreated from the valleys to sit the summits. With a cold wind May snow can fall on the fells. We have had snow as late as the first week in June. But walking in the cool clean air, with the long views still unmarred by the summer haze, is a delight.

May can bring its problems though in the shape of the Spring Bank Holiday, when every car in Britain is on the road, and the long queues of traffic come off the motorway and converge on the National Park.

'Hey, we're in for it!' says the farmer as we discuss the weather prospects for the weekend. 'They'll be walkin' on each other's heads, the weather set fair as it is!'

Come they do. On the Friday night all the camp sites are almost full. By Saturday morning they are and the after-noon comers cannot find a site. Most seek space on the perimeter of the National Park; some just give up and camp on the grass verges. I spend all day answering questions and giving directions. If I stop the Land Rover I am instantly approached.

'Where can I camp?'

'The camp sites are full in the central area. You'll need to move out to the perimeter.'

'But I want to be here!'

A car towing a large caravan trailer is stopped when approaching the narrow steep Blea Tarn road out of Great Langdale, a queue of traffic behind.

'You can't possibly get up that narrow steep road with that trailer,' I advise. 'Where are you aiming for?'

'I'm looking for a trailer caravan site.'

'There isn't one in this valley.'

The driver looked out incredulously to the long green

farm meadows patterned by drystone walls and framed by the ring of superb mountains. He waves his hand towards it all.

'But there is all that – that – dead land!'

Several of us, aided by frustrated motorists, disconnect the trailer and turn it round. Somehow the traffic scrapes past and we set the caravan off on its return journey.

'Oh no!' exclaims a colleague. Half a mile down the road another large trailer caravan is approaching.

There is an old taxi-cab in a field of growing hay. A group of young people are busily erecting a large tent.

'I'm sorry, you'll have to come out of there,' I say.

'Why?' asks a large youth who appears to be in charge of the operation.

'You haven't asked the landowner's permission, and you're damaging a growing crop.'

'This is only grass and we're doing no harm.'

'You're destroying food for stock. Best come on out of it quickly!'

An aggressive little pretty girl, with hair tied in pigtails, leaves the group and stares at me.

'And who the hell are you?'

'National Park Warden.'

'Lay off Jeannie!' – a warning voice from the rear of the group. But Jeannie has not finished. She is working up to an angry flush.

'You're just a pig. A little bourgeois pig. A – a – petty bourgeois lackey of a – a – neo-fascist, paramilitary junta!'

I tell her that I like that and I hope that she will not mind if I write it down at once so that I won't forget it. Particularly the junta bit. I take out my notebook. Everyone's entitled to their opinion, I say, but point out that they are still destroying food, and someone's livelihood. They surely did not want to do that.

'Come on Jeannie! Let's go somewhere else!' The voice from the back.

They are re-packing their tent and gear is being put in the taxi. I give them a leaflet with a list of sites.

'Pig!' calls Jeannie as they drive away.

'Goodbye Jeannie!'

By mid-afternoon I have handed out all my stock of camp-site leaflets and I am getting slightly hoarse. And still they come.

'I've come all the way from Australia!' An irate elderly man. 'Nobody's going to stop me from camping where I want to!'

I explain that if he has come all the way from Australia he surely should not object to driving another fifteen miles to a camp site. And he, if no one else, should surely understand that this is hill sheep farm country and every bit of grass counts. But only one tent! I explain that when other people see his tent they will flock in thinking it is a regular site.

'You'll have to forcibly evict me!' says another irate camper on private land. I tell him that this can certainly be arranged with the support of the farmer, and a police officer standing by to see fair play. But the way things are going it would probably be around one o'clock in the morning by the time we got round to him, everyone being so busy. He says rude things and starts to dismantle his tent.

'But if we only stay here one night?' asks one caravan owner. 'Surely we're doing no harm?'

I ask them what their sanitary arrangements are. Lamely they suggest that they will drive to the nearest public lavatories. Five miles? They get the point and agree to move to a perimeter site.

'It's disgraceful!' announces another trespasser. 'There aren't enough sites!' There are, I explain, sites outside the central area.

206

'But we want to be near the lake shore!' So do many many hundreds of others, I say. What a mess the lake shore would look if it was covered in tents from end to end.

Many people ask the way, showing me the addresses of guest houses and hotels. Why do they not include directions and sketch maps with their pretty brochures? Occasionally a nice problem question arises like, 'My son is camping near Windermere with his school. Where is the site?' Address? They do not know the address. I take them into the mobile information unit, give them a camp site leaflet and star those that are taking school parties.

'Telephone the sites and ask if your son's school is staying there. Then come back here and the information assistant will tell you how to get there.' I spend ten minutes helping the information assistant to deal with his queue of inquiries, then move on.

The prize question has strangely cropped up on a number of occasions. Example: I am approached by a nervous motorist at the Blea Tarn road. He flags me down. Time: fifteen hundred hours.

'Can you help me? I've lost my camp site.'

'Tell me about it.'

'We drove into the Lake District this morning. We'd no idea where to camp but we found ourselves following a car with camping equipment on his roof rack. He seemed to know where he was going, so we followed him. We followed him right to a site and pitched near him. We unpacked everything into the tent then we went off shopping for the weekend food. We drove about six or seven miles, I think, to a village and stocked up, and then we couldn't remember the way we'd come.'

'You don't know the name of the site?'

'No.'

'Valley?'

207

'No.'

'Name of the village where you did the shopping?'

'No. We didn't see a name written up anywhere. It was quite small.'

'Can you describe the site?'

'It's a big field approached by a rough road.'

I describe the entrances to some of the possible sites and he shakes his head miserably. Then I go through the list again describing the area round the sites. When I eventually describe a shop outside one site entrance his face lights up and there is a gasp of relief. He calls to his wife.

'He's got it, Mary!' and to me, 'God! I've asked dozens of people.'

I take no chances. I tell him to get in his car and follow me. Pulling up outside the site gate at Baysbrown I look back and he is flashing the car headlights and sounding his horn and his wife waves delightedly from a window. They must have driven past the site more than once in their search, but the tents are hidden by the trees.

I am stopped by another motorist.

'Can you help me?'

'I hope so.'

'I've lost my wife!' He looks very worried indeed. He is young. Perhaps they have just been married.

'I'm afraid – in case she's been abducted!'

'Tell me about it.'

The man explains. They were in the car towing their caravan and looking for the site at which they had made a provisional telephone booking. Unfortunately in a queue of traffic he overshot a site entrance. He was unable to turn round and, fearful that his place in the site would be taken up if it was not claimed right away, he took advantage of a traffic hold-up to allow his wife to jump out and go back to the site office to make sure of the pitch. He drove on to turn round. It was four miles or more before he managed the turn. He then returned to the site and asked at the office if his wife had been in. He described her. Yes, she had, but she hadn't stopped to make an inquiry; she had climbed into a passing car and left. The car appeared to go in the direction of the village.

'I dropped the caravan off and I've driven up and down, but it's utter madness! She's just vanished.'

I suggest that he park his car, climb into the Land Rover with me and we drive off to the village.

'Is this the way you went with the caravan to turn round?'

'Yes.'

'I reckon she got in the car to chase after you.'

The man is in a state and I do not know what to do with him. I just hope we get a glimpse of her in the village. But we do not reach the village centre. For there she is standing on the grass verge near the village approach looking very worried indeed. I stop, the man jumps out, and the reunion is in the best Hollywood tradition. Definitely recently married.

As I drive them back to their car she explains all. When she got off at the caravan site she realised at once that it was not the site at which they had booked. She rushed out in an effort to catch her husband before he drove on but it was too late. A car was leaving the site and she asked the driver if he was going in the same direction. He was and he gave her a lift. However they failed to find the car and caravan. She asked to be dropped at the village boundary as she was sure that her husband would not drive past her without seeing her if he was coming back. But he had in fact returned by a parallel route on another road.

The telephone is ringing when I eventually get home. More inquiries about sites. Two complaints from farmers.

Colleagues ring in for advice and instructions. A complaint from a landowner. I am gradually making a list for my attention on the following day.

Next day many of the road lay-bys are occupied by campers or car-sleepers. By the busy main road unabashed men in trousers and vests are shaving with the help of their wing-mirrors. One man, seemingly oblivious of the passing traffic, is sitting on the grass verge – cutting his toe nails.

When the pressure is on much of the duty is with police work. I cannot be happy with police work. The essence of enjoyment on a holiday is freedom. 'I may be a wage slave on Monday – but I am a free man on Sunday' – so goes the song of the Manchester rambler, the formidable man of the thirties who was willing to fight the gamekeepers of the big landowners on the Derbyshire moors for the right to roam the hills. It was they who piled on the pressure to compel the government to produce national park legislation.

We all need to throw off the shackles for a time, flee from servitude, and enjoy the freedom of the outdoors. I think that the planning officers, the land owners, foresters and the farmers do a fairly good job of conserving the National Park even if they do not always work together as they should. What has not been done effectively is to reconcile the differences which can arise between the users, the recreationists, and the conservationists.

John Stuart Mill expressed the matter perfectly when he said, 'The liberty of the individual must be thus far limited: he must not make himself a nuisance to other people.' The by-laws, and the other laws we enforce sometimes, are against nuisance. No one must endanger the livelihood of someone else. No one should spoil others' enjoyment.

So we persuade people away from private land to camp sites. And in May we must persuade people with dogs to control them among sheep, especially in the lambing fields.

It is the first grumble of the fell farmer that visitors will not, or more often cannot, control their dogs. The savaging of sheep is fairly rare. The chasing of sheep is very common and can be fatal when sheep are driven into becks or over crags, or a chased ewe in lamb aborts. The persuasion one has to use is normally successful, and most people approached put their dogs on leads. A quiet word is enough. Sometimes it is necessary to shout at an offender over a long distance. That is nasty.

You must never insult a man's dog. Tact is required. The answer to 'My dog is obedience-trained and never gives any trouble. I needn't use a lead,' is 'I'm sure you're right, but please would you mind putting your dog on a lead as an example to other people who have dogs that aren't well trained?' and if they say 'I don't carry a lead,' the answer is 'Oh, hang on. I have a length of twine in my pocket.'

There are some by-laws which might seem superficial. It is forbidden, for instance, to roll or throw stones down fell sides. In fact people are seriously injured and sometimes killed by falling stones. Few stones are dislodged naturally in the summer. They might be knocked down accidentally. They are often thrown down for a lark. The biggest rockfall I observed from near quarters, started by a youth on the summit ridge, was in Buttermere. We were instructing some young people in rock-climbing in Burtness Combe, when one of my colleagues, approaching the crag shouted at the youth, then shouted to us, 'Below!' – the warning that something was on its way down. A rock about the size of a football came first, bouncing high off the crag, then followed some 'grapeshot' that it had dislodged, then there was an ominous sliding sound and boulders came bouncing down. There was a young lady leading a climb on a nearby pitch. We shouted to her and she flattened herself against the crag as a great rock, the size of an upright piano, hit the crag above her. I saw sparks flying, and smelled the hot rock. By good fortune it passed over the girl and her companions and hit the base of the crag, scattering our people who were on the approach. I watched her and she immediately began climbing again, coolly working out her moves. I saw her later on the ridge and congratulated her on keeping her composure.

'Look,' she said, 'I was scared stiff. I had to get to a belay quick and tie on, then wait till my knees stopped knocking. If you catch up with that maniac who started the rock fall – just let me get at him!'

There are by-laws against excessive noise. This is a difficult area. What is excessive? Some activity is completely against the spirit of the National Park. 'People need … the quietness of unspoiled country.' So why international speedboat trials on Windermere? When one of the organisers was asked 'Why Windermere?' his reply, with a shrug, was 'Because Windermere is the ideal place for it.' When military jet aircraft practice noisy low-flying techniques, we are told that the open countryside and the national parks are used because there are no concentrations of population there! Perhaps there are not enough people to complain?

Those who enjoy the national parks in the way that was intended seldom cause us trouble; they include anglers, sailing boat owners, canoists, sail-surfers, swimmers, amateur naturalists, photographers and artists, cyclists, enlightened walkers high and low, and climbers.

I suppose the man who is the perfect example of what a national park is all about, is the seeker of solitude. It is said that there was a notice at one time in the old offices of the National Parks Commission: 'National Parks – Solitude for the Masses.' In fact it is possible in the Lake District, even at the height of a mass invasion, when it seems every car in the country is jammed into every road, to find solitude only a ten-minute walk away from the traffic stream. Most people are gregarious. It is as well for the loners that they are. The man who enjoys the most freedom is the anathema of the mountain rescue teams and the promotors of mountain safety – the lone fell walker with a tent on his back, with maybe only a hazy plan of where he might go. Generally I would advise anyone against doing it alone, especially in winter. But if a man or woman has served an apprenticeship as a fell walker and a camper, I would wish him luck. It is possible to make an assessment of a person's capabilities just by looking at his clothing, how it has been chosen, how it fits and how it has weathered; the way he places his feet as he walks, and the way his rucksack is packed. And his face, whether tense, taxed, or relaxed. If he passes the visual test and my path crosses his I would greet him but I certainly would not question him.

It should not be assumed, however, that the lone walker with a tent is necessarily a responsible user of the countryside. Popular fell camp sites such as Angle Tarn, Stickle Tarn, and Styhead Tarn are constantly fouled by litter. This is particularly aggravating as some volunteer has to clean up and hump all the muck down to the valley – a long way.

We sometimes leave 'Visiting cards' at unoccupied tents with a friendly message asking the tent owner to respect the area. I remember on one occasion walking down Moasdale to Cockley Beck on a compass bearing, away from any path in thick mist and rain. There was, I thought, a hint of orange colour in the gloom on my right. I moved over and found a lone tent. It could not have been more remote. I called a greeting and a head poked from the flap. I gave the man my card, wished him a happy time, leaving him staring, speechless, with his mouth open. He must have thought that to have found him at that remote spot I had special tent-detecting apparatus. Actually I have on some occasions – my dog will home-in on any tent in the mist.

A voluntary warden must have given another lone camper an even greater surprise. He told me that there was nobody at a tent he found high on the fell, but when he felt around his pockets he had no official visiting card. So he found one of his own cards in his trouser pocket and wrote a note on the back. The volunteer worked for the area gas board and on the front of the card was printed: '– Gas Board. The meter reader called to read your meter and you were not in…'

It would be wrong to give people in the remote areas the idea that they are being watched. Any warden duties on the fell, or anywhere else in the Park for that matter, must be low key. True freedom means escape from authority and that includes encounters with officialdom in any form. I and my men might be regarded as representatives of officialdom and bureaucracy, but it is our duty to 'help the public to enjoy the amenities' to 'promote and assist in the proper enjoyment of the countryside and to encourage good behaviour'. So we are less liable to make an approach than to encourage an approach from the 'customer'.

We must have a soft spot for the solitude seeker, the man who has discarded for a while the trappings of civilisation and is prepared to live simply. The breed is rare. It is a pleasure to meet such a man. It was getting dark and it was one of those days with a great howling riot of a wind flinging showers of rain like steel rods. It rocked and hammered at the Land Rover as I battled up the narrow lonely road to the long hill and the wild exposure of the moor summit crossing. There was a car and trailer caravan parked near the top, with the off-side wheels on the road and the nearside on the grass verge. 'Well,' I thought, 'here he is. The man after my own heart. Not another soul for miles in this remote spot. A man with simple needs.' Then I thought, 'Best call. He might have had a break-down. With such a long haul up this hill his car engine may have overheated or seized?'

The trailer pitched over at each blow from the wind gusts. I stopped. The car was empty but there was a light at the caravan window. I disembarked, pulled up my anorak hood and struggled to the door and knocked. It opened a few inches and I shouted to make myself heard over the din of the storm.

'Are you all right?'

The door opened a little wider and a man looked out, saw the official Land Rover and grinned at me.

'Yes,' he shouted. 'Is it all right if I stay here overnight?'

'Yes,' I shouted in reply, 'but you've picked a wild spot!'

'I know,' he called back, and making a gesture of approval with his hand, 'but the colour television reception is fantastic!'

<hr>

The Oak Wood

My home is a light tent. For simple comfort a sleeping bag, a mat and a candle. Food enough is contained in a small box, food for the mind in a small book. But from my doorway I enjoy pure luxury. There is the best view a retiring character like me could wish for – an oak wood sloping steeply down to green meadows and a winding river. Beyond, the opposite side of the valley, another broadleaved woodland billowing upwards like great clouds of green cumulus. Above that a few fingers of crag. Then the woods give me a wealth of music. In the oak above me a blackbird sings and fills my tent with its song. Somewhere below a song thrush is singing its heart out. As twilight approaches a woodcock or two croak and squeak their mysterious way above me. And there is perfume too – the sweet voluptuous scent of wild hyacinth, for below me the woodland floor, not yet darkened by full summer leaf, is bright blue with them. And I have the luxury of solitude and a sense of wilderness. The only path to my lone camp has been made by deer, and the roebuck, whose territory I have trespassed upon, has already voiced his bad-tempered indignation, long hoarse calls followed by short angry

216

outbursts. At twenty-two hundred hours precisely, an owl cries and is answered down the valley, then another and another.

This is not true wilderness. There is no wilderness left in Britain, if wilderness is defined as a natural environment devoid of human influence. But there is a sense of wilderness here in the broadleaved woodland among the fells of the Lake District and it is very precious. And it is terribly vulnerable.

I lie back on my mat, snuff my candle, and in the dusky twilight that passes for a northern midsummer night I dream an uneasy dream. I dream that threatened by dereliction or destruction the only broadleaved woodland left is suddenly acquired by and shared between three public authorities who recognise its value and independently decide that their own portion shall be a special reserve. For several years, certainly long before workers move in to make good the fences against grazing sheep and repair the damage to the woodland, each authority calls in ecologists and planners and foresters to do surveys and prepare management plans. When all the specialists compromise on their recommendations and the time for decisions actually arrives, each management committee is impressed with the importance of doing the right thing (and hopefully doing it rather better than his neighbour). Some of the committee members, although they devote much of their voluntary time to other committees too, have actually read the reports and recommendations and are prepared to begin. Time goes on.

The first authority is strong on education and feels that there is a great crusading role to play in converting the public to the cause of woodland conservation. It is also aware of the great educational potential of the 'broadleaved woodland environment'. However, the committee realises

217

that, as its officers recommend, it cannot allow the public to wander anywhere in this fragile area, so the obvious thing is to draw them all to an educational centre and confine their excursions into the wood on made-up trails. An educational centre is converted from a Victorian country house which happens to be handy. Dormitory, dining-room and kitchen extensions are built on to accommodate students, and the old coach house is made into a lecture theatre and fitted out with all the modern apparatus for audio-visual presentations. In several rooms of the house exhibitions are laid out with well-lit photographs of what the public can see outside, with detailed captions showing the geology and the human history of the area. There are also specialised exhibits on broadleaved trees, woodland plants peculiar to the area, insects, mammals and birds. It is in fact possible to learn all about the woods around the centre without leaving the building, and in addition to the exhibits there is a well-stocked library. The centre has staff of high academic standing backed by technicians to maintain the sophisticated equipment, and there are administrators, domestics, and caterers.

In the wood nature trails are laid out and the various species of trees are numbered for easy reference. Hides are provided at suitable points overlooking specially made clearings which are favoured by feeding deer. Where the nature trails go through wet areas a plastic based footpath is laid. However students are not entirely confined to the nature trails. In some selected areas they are allowed to take in apparatus to do in-depth assessments of such things as leaf-litter and plant colonies, fungi and ornithology. In one area some felling has been done and replanted to provide a broadleaved arboretum.

In the first years there are worrying and large financial losses and the specially arranged courses were unaccountably undersubscribed. It is decided to advertise them more widely, and to extend their scope to include subjects other than woodland ecology. The centre is much in demand for conferences and special summer schools.

The second authority are above all keen to be tasteful and to help them they have a strong team of planning officers and designers. They have a handy barn. At all costs it must continue to look like a barn in the local idiom. The fact that the barn is derelict and has to be taken down and rebuilt is beside the point. As it is a barn, there is no attempt made to put in windows other than the tiny slots which were there originally, so the whole of the inside is artifically and tastefully floodlit. Being restricted for space inside, and bearing in mind the need to give the visitor a meaningful experience, much thought is given to enlightening design. There is no room for extensive interpretive exhibits and so two themes are displayed: 'The Oak' is the first one, with a fine artistic impression of one covering a whole magnificently lit wall. There are also smaller artistic impressions of 'The Oak through the seasons'. The other theme is 'The Insects of the Oak Wood'. There is little room to cover this in detail, but there is a marvellously blown-up colour picture feature of the oak eggar moth. The building and its interior is instantly given a national design award, followed by a European award.

The centre is very strong on fine illustrated salable leaflets on all aspects of broadleaved woodland ecology. Much of the information is superficial, but no one could fault the design. Outside the building paths lead to carefully staged natural exhibits with beautifully designed interpretive displays colour-etched into sheet alloy and mounted in solid teak frames.

The committee is strong on stating that the purpose of the centre is not to attract more people into the sensitive area. However, it is the authority's showpiece, and many foreign visitors, particularly architects and planners, beat a path to the barn door from the nicely screened car park.

Hardly anyone goes into the wood here. They really don't need to. This is as well, as this authority is not strong on practical woodland maintenance and does not have the staff to do it.

The third authority takes a different view, possibly because its committees sit far away in a northern city, but its advantage is that it is able to call upon a large amount of technical skill and has a larger budget. The Recreation, Cemeteries, Leisure and Countryside Amenities Committee is keen on encouraging the urban dwellers to appreciate the countryside and its natural history. A redundant highway authority yard and workshops in an old quarry are handy to the wood and are purchased. An area is cleared for a large car and coach park. The committee is considerably disturbed when their application for a building of modern design is turned down by the planning authority, but eventually a compromise design is agreed. Above the quarry housing the complex is a good viewpoint and this is cleared of scrub and some unimportant trees, and a picnic area is provided with rustic seats and tables. The committee decides against rustic litter receptacles and there are some routed signs instead exhorting the public to 'Take their litter home'. (Some think that home is rather too far to take it, and their litter is carefully hidden under gorse bushes, birch thickets and under piles of stones.) There is also a 'children's recreation area' set aside, with climbing frames, nets and swings.

In the building the emphasis is on displays with good educational content, easily understandable and entertaining. There are model sailing ships, models of Elizabethan buildings, a live wood-ant colony behind glass, and a working model of a water-powered sawmill. In the theatre there are continuous showings of films and slide sequences on birds and animals of the woodlands. They are light and entertaining. There is a large café serving hot meals or snacks and a shop selling a wide variety of souvenir books, sweets, chocolate and ice cream.

Outside the short-length nature trails are easy to follow and as everything is labelled the leaflet is optional. There is a large hide overlooking a well-made artificial lake and ducks are breeding successfully.

The committee is keen on attendance figures and happy to see them climbing. It can also boast that, unlike its neighbours, the centre is gradually paying for itself. The committee however regrets that planning permission to make a small site for touring caravans in a well-screened area of the wood was refused, even though there is obviously a need for inexpensive self-catering accommodation in this area for those who wish to enjoy all that the woodland and the surrounding countryside can offer.

And how does nature respond to all this human activity? Remarkably well for it is mainly on the fringe. The deer, accustomed to seeing human beings on defined paths, and getting at least some protection by the perimeter fences from the attention of poachers, become almost tame. The fences and paths also protect the badgers from disturbance from the local 'sportsmen' who like to dig them out. Red squirrels are attracted to the food scraps provided by the centres, and regularly visit the bird tables for their rations of peanuts. There is regeneration of the woodland now protected from browsing domestic animals, and the flora is only marginally affected by the small amount of drainage work done. The addition of artificial ponds has diversified the species, and there is dramatic increase in bird numbers.

But it is the effect on the humans that is worrying. Soon

will it not be possible at all to see unfenced nature actually in its raw state? Will it be possible to wander freely and look at and enjoy nature for what it is and without some academic educationist talking over your shoulder about it?

Dreams? They could be exchanged for nightmares. It could be decided that the broadleaved woodland is getting so rare that, with taxpayers' money, it should be enclosed behind high fences and entry only allowed by permit and restricted to people doing serious research work. Or worse, the impoverished land owner, victim of inflationary spirals and high taxation, resolves, with the conditional approval of the Forestry Commission and the planning authority, who are powerless to stop him anyway, to fell all the hardwoods in all the woods, with the exception of a few perimeter areas and some high land, and replant the whole with Sitka spruce for a quick return. This is more likely than anything else.

I dream of a miracle. Could it possibly happen that this wood might be managed and maintained, and just kept as it is? But then I have uneasy thoughts. Do I in the luxurious comfort of my cloth home consider myself among the elite? Why cannot all who want to share the enjoyment of my one-night stay in this neck of the woods also come along to fill the wood with tents? To maintain the sense of wilderness, would a permit system be needed to restrict the numbers? A terrible thought. But is not access to wilderness in most overseas national parks already subject to permit? And permit seekers have to prove that they are experienced and responsible people?

'We shall all have to carry identity cards one day,' complained a keen ornithologist friend seeking access to a reserve.

'Maybe,' I suggested, 'we should all be ringed for life at our fledgeling stage.'

Access by permit is one thing but once inside our 'wilderness' there should be no sign of human management, no interference with privacy. The few maintenance workers should not be conspicuous. The essence of enjoyment of wilderness is solitude and freedom.

My dreams are interrupted by a dawn chorus of birds so loud that I can almost believe myself translated to the gates of paradise. Well – not exactly. It is too much really. The heavenly chorus gets a bit hysterical. First thing in the morning it is something of a general ding-dong and I had better evacuate the tent and see what sort of a morning the birds are shouting about. Ice-cold water from the beck will wash the drowsiness from my eyes. A short walk, and I am sitting high on a rock with legs dangling over the side and there is absolutely no sign anywhere of human presence.

The green frondose clouds of the tree tops below lit with soft yellow light ripple in a soft clean wind. A buzzard uses it to lift off an oak nearby. It merely opens its wings, spread like two great hands, and rises up above me, then by some subtle movement of the body begins to circle. As I watch another rises rapidly to join it and they follow-my-leader round in great curves. But I cannot enjoy the sight for long as there are so many distractions. The loud liquid notes of a tiny wren come from somewhere near my right elbow. It is pure music that drowns the rest. But it is really, I guess, a bad-tempered Wagnerian outburst of indignation at my trespass.

But back to breakfast. I drop the tent, pack all away and when I am gone there will be no sign that I have been. One last look round, a salute to my companions the trees, and a deep hope that they will still be here long long after I have gone forever.

A Mountain Search

I looked across Windermere one sunny Summer morning, fresh after rain, at the Old Man range. Wetherlam, its prominent northern spur, was streaking fingers of cloud. The Old Man range is the most prominent sight from the east of Windermere, a great straggle of volcanic hunchbacks towering above the rounded tree-covered Silurian hills. The range has long been my familiar neighbour. It has welcomed me in all weathers. I did my first rock climbs on Dow Crag, the 350 feet high cliff below one of the lesser peaks. I had picked over the mineral heaps below its abandoned mines for rock specimens, had hunted for plants among the broken crags, quarry faces and ravines. Wetherlam, of all the hills, was a friend.

I was called to the pub at Coniston by the police at two o'clock that afternoon. There was a schoolboy missing on the fell. The local rescue team had searched the mountain paths all morning without success. The boy was thought to have been on the fell all night. There had been heavy rain and strong winds. The police, fearing the worst, decided that advice and reinforcements were needed. A huge area of rough land might have to be searched. So I, with the other members of the Mountain Search Advisory Panel, consisting of team leaders from all the Lake District Mountain Rescue units, had been called in to assist. The chairman of the panel, a veteran of many rescues and searches, called us to order and asked the police inspector to speak. He thanked us for our attendance, then started to explain. The lad, aged sixteen, was a member of a school party staying at the local hostel. The previous day the party had set off to climb Coniston Old Man. The missing lad had complained of feeling ill and had been sent down. That was the last the party saw of him. He had not been reported missing until this morning. The Inspector suggested that we should have the teacher in at once. He was waiting in another room.

The young teacher came in, his face looking drawn and worried; he stammered some apologies for causing us so much trouble. He really did not know for sure if the boy was on the fell at all, but he was becoming more and more certain that he was.

The party, of seventeen boys and girls with two teachers, had set off in the fine clear weather of the previous morning, to climb the fell by way of Goat's Water. The missing boy, Allan, complained of feeling unwell and began to lag behind. The teacher pointed to the village which could be seen clearly, and told him to walk slowly down to it and wait at the hostel. The lad had not appeared to be happy with the suggestion but had set off down the hill.

The boy was not at the hostel when they returned. However, the hostel warden had certainly seen him talking to a motorist in the village in the early afternoon. The teachers were a bit concerned when Allan did not appear for supper, but concluded that he had had a fit of the sulks and had started to hitch-hike home. His parents were warned and asked to keep a watch for him.

When the parents were telephoned again the following

morning (that was this morning), the teacher was told that he had not reached home but a letter from him, posted on the previous afternoon, had. The letter certainly did not suggest a fit of the sulks, or an intention to return home. The teachers became worried and went to the police who called out the local rescue team.

'Tell us about the boy,' said the chairman. 'Was he likely to have gone back up the fell if he had begun to feel better?'

'It's out of character for him to disobey an instruction. He's a sensible and good lad. I told him to wait at the hostel. He's subject to asthma attacks which sometimes might be brought on by anxiety. They often go as quickly as they come.'

'Why didn't you think of sending someone else down with him?'

'It was a fine clear morning. You could see the village and the route all the way down. It was a pity to spoil someone else's day.'

'Did the lad know the route the party was taking?' someone else asked.

'I think he did. The route was all on the well-trodden paths and finished on Wetherlam, the descent being by Lad Stones.'

The chairman asked the teacher to leave and we considered the situation. We have heard the same story so often. One member of a party is the outsider. Sick or tired or unpopular, he or she is often told to sit by a rock and not to move until the party returns by the same route to pick him up. On the return the person is not there. Possibly the estimated time of pick-up was optimistic and he or she got tired, or alarmed, at waiting alone in the fog. Sometimes the party would return on a parallel route and completely miss contact. We have heard the tale so many times; this was just a variation on a theme. The worried leader of a group

226

always told us the tale as if it was the most amazing and unique thing that had ever happened.

The local rescue team leader took up the story and we gathered round the large-scale maps. It had rained on and off all morning, clearing about noon. The team had been called out at 9.30 and had immediately begun a search of the paths on the school party's route. They had searched an area on both sides of the paths. The route had been drawn on the map. His team was still out, now doing the same journey in reverse.

'From your local knowledge have you any hunches?' asked the chairman.

'I have a strong feeling that he's on the fell. But it's very difficult. If he's been benighted he could be anywhere. As you know, it's extremely rough ground. And there's the old quarry faces, and the scores and scores of old mine shafts, some almost invisible in high bracken. Then there's last night's weather. Gusty wind and rain.'

The constable went out and returned with copies of photographs of the boy obtained by police headquarters. The lad was tall and lean, with a long austere face.

'What was he wearing?'

There were groans as we were told 'an olive-green anorak and dark trousers'. His brown rucksack was missing. He was ideally camouflaged. From the large-scale maps we decided where further searches were to be concentrated. Assuming more help was with us within one hour, we had about six and a half hours of good light. The weather forecast promised clearer weather followed by more rain. There would be no moon that night. We began to call out more of the nearby teams at once, and reinforcements from outlying teams which we could reasonably expect to reach us in the late afternoon and early evening.

I picked up half a dozen volunteers at once. We decided

227

to concentrate a search on the main beck in case the lad had been swept downstream when trying to cross it. In view of the depth of the water caused by the downpour, this was a possibility. The beck tore down a ravine in a series of falls and we clambered down the slimy rock and searched the ledges and hollows on either side. It was very tricky indeed. If we had fallen into the ghyll we could have been swept downstream. I was glad I had put on an old pair of nailed boots. They were ideal on the slippery surface and were fairly waterproof. Not that waterproofing mattered though after an hour of scrambling: to negotiate some sections of the twisting ravine it was necessary to wade in to knee depth. The noise of the falling water was deafening and we could only communicate with each other by sign language.

After an hour and a half we were near the ghyll foot and I waved the party out. There was a sudden shout and Jimmy, a mature man of long experience, was seen to be up to his waist in fast water, hanging onto a holly root for his life and laughing wildly. In a flash his brother Dave was sitting on the holly; he uncoiled his rope and passed a bowline round Jimmy's chest. 'Come on out, you silly – ,' he shouted, and the pair struggled out and up the bank.

On return to search base, which had now been established in the youth hostel on the fell side, we were told that more reinforcements were on the way. The object was now to make the search over and about every known footpath on the fell. Each team had been allotted a search area. Evening reinforcements from my own team had been told to meet at Tilberthwaite to tackle the fell from the north side, and I suggested to the search leader that I should join them. I drove my Land Rover down the rough track and had to dodge three others bounding up loaded with men. I drove round to our meeting point at an old quarry tip, changed into dry boots and socks, ate a sandwich and drank some coffee. It was now a beautiful evening, still and quiet, except for the muffled sound of falling water from the ghyll. There was no wind, no movement in the larches which grew around the quarry base, just a solitary buzzard wheeling high above them in the blue sky. I wondered idly if the sharp eyes of the bird from that height could see the lad lying in some hollow perhaps, or half-hidden in bracken?

I resorted to my rucksack, made sure that I had spare food in it and checked that my torch was working. I walked round the corner and looked upwards at the great rocks, the water cascading down the slash of ravine, a geological fault, with every near-vertical face of it sprouting growth of larch, ash and yew. Most of the trees were self-sown. Who planted the first larch? Perhaps the miners, needing pit props for the copper mines high above. I swept the view with my binoculars. Way up high there were grazing sheep, some seemingly poised on impossible ledges. I swept slowly left to right, down and right to left. I tried one loud shout of the boy's name. There was one echo, a moment when the only sound was the falling water, then back and to my left another echo. I strained my ears.

I walked back to the Land Rover and soon I heard the sound of approaching cars, engines changing notes as drivers went up and down gears on the winding road. The team was arriving. I spread out the map on the bonnet, pinning it down with four pieces of prime quarry slate and waited for the team leader, Bryan, to join me. He was in the second car and I showed him our search area.

'That goes high,' he said. 'Best waste no time.'

We decided to split the team into two groups of ten, each with a leader, one group on either side of the ghyll. The area was a bit hazardous with paths on both sides but some looseness. I joined the left-hand team and went well out on the flank so that I could cover a wide field outside as well as inside the search area with my binoculars. The inside group members worked more slowly as they were scrambling in and out of the ghyll.

The fascination of mountains is that they are never the same. They change character with the weather, the visibility, the season, and your feeling of atmosphere depends upon fitness and your mood. In a search it almost appears that the fell is playing a game with us, a cunning game of find-the-thimble? No, something more sinister, perhaps. 'I have struck the man down. Now find him if you can.' He might be injured, he might be dead. The Lake District fells by their nature are incredibly hard to search. The volcanic rocks of the central fells are gnarled and shattered and gullied. It is possible to walk within a few feet of a recumbent person without seeing him. If he falls and rolls he is almost bound to stop in a hollow. Add to that bracken, great seas of it anything up to five feet high, and the task seems almost impossible. It is not only necessary to search ahead, but to stop regularly to look back at the ground you have passed.

The most difficult job of a search group leader is keeping his men working together. In a line search the line must somehow keep straight. The end markers play a key role, but it is the leader's job to call out if the line gets dog-legged. Now if, as in this case, one part of the team is on very difficult ground, the more fortunate searchers on better terrain have to go slowly and wait for them. The next important job for the leader is to make sure that everyone is actually searching and is not too preoccupied with finding his own way. He must know at any time where he is on the map, bearing in mind the total search area.

The search was a slow business as it was necessary to explore every corner of the deep ravine. An anorak was found in the depths and passed along the line to Bryan. It was obviously an old one and had been lying there for a year at least. At the top of the ghyll we were on relatively easier terrain – a broad step on the high fell side. We found radio contact here – previously we had been shielded from contact by the fell – and reported our position. But the hazards here were knee-high bracken and some old mine shafts and workings. One shaft was brim-full with crystal-clear water, perhaps a hundred or more feet deep. It was so clear that when I dropped slate in the water it was possible to watch it slowly sinking, drifting from side to side as it went. We reached the end of the search area and searched the broken walls of buildings, then set off in a sweep downwards back to our vehicles. When we got well down the light was beginning to go. We managed another signal to base and were told that we were to go home when we had finished; the team leader was to phone in for instructions, if any, the following day. The last yards down to the road were done at a run. We could still get to the pub before closing time.

I phoned base at seven the following morning and was told to rejoin. It had showered again in the night and there was some drifting cloud on the mountain. I ate my break-fast, such as it was, on the Windermere ferry and drove on to Coniston and the youth hostel on the fell. The day's search had started and several groups were already on the mountain. Some had been out all night. I looked down the road and could see vehicles grinding their way up. One car I recognised as belonging to a local newspaper reporter. Others following were likely of the same calling. There appeared to be some police 'brass' on the way up too, and several police vans. 'Dogs and handlers from headquarters,' I was told.

An ex-army lorry dropped off some fifteen young men; the new search leader told me that these lads who were 'outward bounders' were all mine for the search. We were joined by some young men from a local YMCA camp, which gave me twenty-three in all. I went into search headquarters where an old miner was advising on dangerous shafts.

'How many holes are there?' he was asked.

'Why man,' he answered, 'the fell is as full of holes as a maggoty old cheese.'

I was told I was to search, for the third time, along the main route to the summit. But this time I was to make it very thorough.

'Let's have 'em almost touching hands through that high bracken. Make it good. Get as far as the rock gap then sweep back.'

I was allocated one very large policeman with a very large German shepherd dog which was his working partner. The officer told me that he had never been on a mountain in his life before, so not to overdo it on speed. I asked if the dog should be in front. Yes, it should. What were the chances of it finding after so long?

'This dog,' the officer said, 'works in a city and it's so used to sorting out trouble in pubs that it practically goes berserk when it smells beer. Now if the lad's lying up there and he's supped alcohol in the last three days, it'll find him and sit on him till I get there.'

I strung the lads out to the right of the path after telling them what was expected of them. An experienced team member offered to come along with us and act as my end marker. Searching in wet bracken is a terrible job. It is like wading in water to the waist and the activity stirs up persistent flies. Bracken is tough and wiry and does its best to trip and grab at you. It is difficult to see down into bracken, you could practically stand on a man before you saw him. The police officer was having a very rough time

232

and his language was colourful. The progress of the dog could be seen by the moving bracken in front and we could only guess what he was making of this alien environment.

We reached the rock gap by mid-morning and had a rest. We had no radio so I could not report my position. One always wonders on these occasions if, unknown to us, there has been a find and the search is off. But high above on the fell I could see another search party diligently searching. They would certainly have contact with base.

The police officer, covered in sweat and wet through, drained a flask and said, 'I thought mountains were all rocks and heather, not covered in this mucky fern. God, if the wife could see me now!'

The dog's tongue was hanging out and it was making steam-engine noises, occasionally stopping to snap at the swarm of flies.

We lined up again higher up the fell and began to sweep back. Then the rain came. There was good deal of blue sky so this was just a shower, but it put an even greater damper on the proceedings. It was difficult to make sure that everyone was actually searching all the time and I had to keep up exhortations. It was a great relief to get to the end of the search area. When I called to my searchers 'back to base!' everyone rushed off, the drooling prospect of food and refreshment causing a near stampede. I let them go and continued with dog and handler at our leisure. I was feeling the strain.

I had my sandwiches and soup at headquarters and was briefed for my afternoon assignment. All the known routes had been searched at least once. A team of local men who knew the old mine workings were looking in dangerous holes and abandoned shafts. I was told to take the team of lads I had had that morning (minus the dog and handler), supplemented with a few mountain rescue men who had been resting; we were to sweep the sides of the valley below the line from Wetherlam which the school party had descended. It had been searched before but with fewer men. This time we had to do it thoroughly and slowly. It was an extremely difficult areas with crags, hollows, bogs, deep bracken, and old mine shafts. There were a number of paths too, and quite a few sheep trods. I asked the search controller if he was sure the lad was on the fell. He nodded.

'I think so. But we're running short on ideas. If you think of any let us know.'

I decided to start high with my first line sweep on the southern side of the valley, sweep back at a lower level, then repeat the technique on the other side. I asked Dick, one of the long-experienced adults, to take a high point because he had a good pair of binoculars. The lower marker was Pop, a veteran mountaineer whose fitness belied his years. It took us about forty minutes to line-up for the first sweep and a heavy shower of rain did little to encourage us. By the time we had spread ourselves out, however, there were shafts of sunlight breaking through the cloud and the visibility below us was good. I was in a position somewhat higher than centre with a radio and the operator, Ron, at my elbow. When I was satisfied with the line I waved my arm, Pop and Dick acknowledged and we all moved forward. I nodded to Ron.

'Base from Tango One, commencing search – over.'

'Tango One from Base. Roger. Out.'

We heard the other groups calling base to report movement.

We were faced on the contouring walk with crag outcrops, blocks of rock, some of them unstable, and wet bracken up to three feet high in places. There was a shout of 'Below!' as one of the searchers above dislodged a rock which bounced down the line and sent everyone scattering

234

for cover. 'Take care!' I yelled. The warning was repeated by Pop with some forceful embellishments. When one part of the line was slowed down by some physical impediment, Pop, Dick and I had to call out to the searchers on easier contours to hold back. Ron and I soon met one of the difficulties – a wet, moss-covered crag face with a slippery sloping ledge. We followed it in the hope that it would run out into the fell beyond, but it narrowed. Seeing a movement above my head, I looked into the wild slit-eyes of a handsome young fox who was peering from a clump of holly. I signalled to Ron and we both stared at the animal which appeared to be examining us with uncertain disbelief, but strangely made no attempt to move away. But we had to slither back the way we had come and onto safer ground. We both walked below the crag and the waiting line moved off again.

'Keep looking!' called Pop. 'Come on lads, you aren't out for a stroll. Keep your eyes peeled. You're supposed to be searching!'

This seemed to have some effect for a lad above me shouted and pointed at the opposite side of the valley. I saw with some excitement what he was indicating. It was a patch of lighter green among the dark green of the bracken. But it was a long way off. I called to Dick and pointed. We all waited with caught breath.

'That must be him!' someone called. Dick focused his binoculars.

'It's a patch of sphagnum!' he called down and waved his arm forward. We continued the search, but somehow the false alarm made us all more alert. Calls were coming up and arms waving and we looked at distant shapes and colours which proved to be sheep, more patches of light-coloured bog, juniper bushes, one distant lone walker who had stopped for refreshment, a piece of old aircraft

235

wreckage.

We were beginning to plod again through some particularly difficult block scree when a searcher just below me called and pointed to the other side of the valley, but low down. Now everyone was shouting and Dick called 'Yes!' Pop was calling wildly for everyone to keep the line, but by this time whistles were blowing and there was a general rapid movement down the hill. I nodded to Ron.

'Base from Tango One. Urgent. Urgent message. Find. I say again. Find. Wait – over.'

'Tango One from Base. Roger. Waiting message. Out to you. All search teams. All search teams from Base. Stop searching. Hold your position and wait. I repeat...'

Now Ron and I were hurrying down to the valley floor. Stan, another of the adult searchers, was with the casualty and my spirits sank as I saw him waving everyone back. As we approached he gave me the thumbs-down sign. I picked out ten of the stronger looking lads for stretcher bearing and ordered the rest down to base under Pop's care.

'Thanks lads, you've done a grand job. Don't speak to anyone! Just report to your chief instructor and leader when you get back.'

I looked at our casualty. He had been dead for some time, and was straggled out like a stringless puppet. No sign of injury. Surprisingly, he was very near a path which must have been used by searchers earlier, but he was hidden by bracken, hence it had been easier to spot him from above. Ron was radioing for a stretcher. I gave him the code word for 'fatality'. At this stage it was undesirable to let it be known that the lad was dead for there was no telling who was in earshot of the base radio. His parents would need to be told first.

As we listened to base calling all the teams in we sat silently. Most of us were some respectable distance away. I

236

tried to imagine why the boy had finished his life here. He had obviously gone back up the fell against orders to try to meet the party, but he had taken a path in the valley bottom, a long way from the ridge which the true route followed. As Stan was an ambulance superintendent with long experience of accidents of all sorts, I asked him his opinion.

'Probably fell over, only a few feet but enough to knock himself out. He may have had a blackout or something. Then by the awkward way he was lying on the slope he may have suffocated. What a tragedy! A nice lad like that.'

The stretcher arrived with a team of sweating men. We waited until a constable and the doctor joined us. Photographs were taken as evidence for the inquest, and the casualty was then carefully laid on the stretcher, covered, and strapped in.

Carrying a stretcher down a fell side is very hard work for the ground is extremely rough. To begin with the path is too narrow. It will only take one man in comfort. The front and back stretcher-bearers fitted in the carrying harness are on the path. The six side bearers are on either side, struggling on rough blocks of rock, or in bracken, or scrabbling for a hold on falling ground while still trying to bear a share of weight. If a man stumbles or falls he lets go, picks himself up and takes the weight again. It is a sort of mad dance. The front members shout back to warn the rear of obstacles. There is inevitably chatter –not so much if a man is badly injured, for then the carry is slow with stops so that the patient's condition can be regularly checked and treatment given. But if a man is just lightly injured – or if he is dead – the only thoughts are to get down in one piece without wasting time. Initiates to rescue might think the team callous when handling a fatality. But there are few, if any, of the rescue team who are not upset at dealing with

237

death, particularly if the victim is a young person. There is hardly any keen fell walker or climber who cannot honestly feel that 'there, but for the grace of God, go I'. Chatter relieves tension. It helps to get on with the job. So there is speculation about getting down to the valley before closing time, insults about members being overweight, and accusations of over indulgence in the sins of the flesh, bad language and laughter as bearers take tumbles.

At regular intervals the carrying team is changed. We were in fact close to an improved area of the route, where the rough path joined an old mine track, when the sweating carriers changed over for the last time. I surrendered my place to a fresh man, and unusually the police constable who had been walking with us took the front, put the carrying harness over his shoulders and we set off again. After the descent of a hundred yards or so we saw some people coming up the mine track to meet us. One seemed to be a man in late middle age, wearing a suit, and stumbling in city shoes. The constable, struggling in the harness, swore loudly.

'That's the lad's father! Who let him come on up here? He likely doesn't know. He can't know!' He turned to me.

'Get down there! Get him down to the mine buildings.'

He saw my look of horror.

'Go on man! Run!' and turning round, 'Keep your voices down lads.'

I ran, jumping from rock to rock, and I reached the group. I looked at the father's face, haggard, white. He was not a young man. His only child had come to him late. I was completely out of breath, and anyway could not think of anything to say. He met my eyes. I took his sleeve and could still say nothing. I suppose I was trying to turn him away. He looked hard at me for what appeared to be a long time and then, reading what must have been obvious, his mouth opened and he uttered a loud wail of shock and anguish that tore me apart. He turned with me and we walked down. I was gripping his jacket to hold him up and he was staggering and leaning heavily. It was almost as if I could feel the deep pain coming through and out of him. He began to repeat, 'Oh dear God! My boy! My boy!' loudly, then more softly as we descended. And I know what it is to find suddenly that all your hopes, the main reason for living, has left you. I took him down to the hostel by the mine buildings, steering him away from the press and sightseers. The hostel warden showed us into a private room. I sat him down. I did not know what else to do. I did not want to leave him but we were now among concerned people. A lady from the Womens' Voluntary Service Corps gave him a cup of tea; although the room was warm he was hunched and shivering. Other kind people came in. I just touched his shoulder and walked away.

I went to the mines hut to await the stretcher, to help to keep the gathering sightseers back and to prepare a statement. But thoughts kept running back to the hunched figure. I had a conscience about leaving him. A man with only memories left, what must seem an utterly empty future, and the huge question why, that no one, no matter how sympathetic, can ever answer for him. And I thought of the words of sympathy that well-meaning people would be speaking, and how useless and meaningless it would all seem.

There was another 'casualty' too. I had a glimpse of the teacher in charge. He must have been torturing himself with the knowledge that if he had sent someone down the mountain with the boy the tragedy would not have happened. His face was deathly white and taut.

An hour or so later I was looking back again at the view of the mountain framed by the trees of home. It looked as

239

beautiful as ever, the shadows picking out the crags, the cool evening wind moving a halo of thin white cloud from the summit into the pale blue sky. It was as beautiful as ever. Sometimes in the evening silence after a day of work and worry the view is a great comfort. The mountain says, 'Hold still' and in a moment all the tensions that man is heir to seem petty, and they slip away. The mountain looked as beautiful as ever, but what did it say tonight? I could hear the anguished voice of the father. I could hear nothing else. I could read no other message. Nothing. The mountain shed no tears.

Flowers

Every year I think, 'Surely this is the best year ever for flowers.' Every hedgerow, every field, every wood, every river bank and swamp is bright with flowers of every colour. Species flourish in cycles. You may have an average year for daffodils, but later on, every bush of broom is alight with gold. But there are special years when many species enjoy their abundance, so each year has its extra special favour. 1979 was surely the year of the honeysuckle. The flowering came late, but then every clambering, straggling, clinging spread of it was choked with blossom, and the evening air, particularly after rain, was heavy with its exquisite perfume, mingling with the scent of the meadowsweet and the more subtle scent of wild rose.

There are July riches in abundance as soon as I leave my front door. First there is the distant view towards the wood. Since the felling there last season, the grass has grown lush and is bright pink and purple, a strange Disney cartoon colour rippling like liquid in the wind. The grasses with the extraordinary colours are the bents, and the pink downy Yorkshire fog. Strange name. Has it anything to do with the rosy pink view of life that Yorkshire folk have after Sunday

241

dinner with two helpings of Yorkshire pudding, roast beef and apple pie and cream? Apparently not, for the name probably comes from *fogg*, a Norse name for grass. Beyond the tall spikes of the luxurious cow parsleys, across the meadow still smelling sweet after the hay-cut, the beck banks are bright with colour. Purple knapweed, vetch, loosestrife, mauve valerian, red hemp agrimony, campion, ragged robin and burnet, pale blue harebell, yellow butter-cups, St John's wort, birdsfoot-trefoil, yellow loosestrife, white meadow-sweet, bedstraw, ox-eye daisy, yarrow and tall hogweeds. Within a small area there is a riot of species all shouting for attention from the bees and the hoverflies, and the more discriminating butterflies and moths. Beyond are the reed beds; I watch as a sudden breeze through the tree tops calls the faithful to prayer and the whole mass sighs and bows down to the east as one.

I take a guided party from Brockhole up a nearby lane. Nothing extraordinary about the lane but still a lot to see. I point out that in olden days every plant was very familiar to the countryfolk because it was from them that they sought food, medicine and ointment. I stop my party a short way up the track and without moving I point out nettles – the new shoots of which were boiled as a spring vegetable. I have had them myself, plunged into boiling salted water for only a few minutes, then strained and chopped with butter and pepper. The fibres of mature plants were thrashed out and used to spin and weave a coarse cloth. Elder – a very special tree – was considered a fairy tree which warded off evil. Its green spring shoots were boiled as a vegetable in lean times, the flowers were used in ointments and lotions, and the berries were eaten; sometimes they were used as a substitute for currants in cakes, or to make wine. Every part of the plant – root, bark, flowers berries and leaves – was used in medicine. Elderberries are still popular with home wine makers, and elderflower champagne is a favourite summer non-intoxicating drink.

Nearby is tall yellow St John's wort, another magic herb used to ward off witches, ghosts and bad luck. It was once hung above cottage doors, or worn as a charm. Two more yellow herbs at our feet, the ubiquitous tormentil, everywhere in the Lake District – even on the high fells – and tiny yellow flowers with strawberry-like leaves, once used to cure the 'torments', whatever they were. Were they used as a pain killer? And then there is herb bennet, that common plant with the small spherical hooked seed-heads which are easily picked up by animals and people's clothing This is the old herbalist's *herba benedicta* the blessed herb; it was associated with St Benedict (St Bennet) and its aromatic root gives the flavour to the liqueur benedictine. Herb robert, again very common locally, is growing on the wall. This is a geranium which can be readily seen from its cranesbill like seed-heads. It is one of my favourites because it blooms from spring to autumn, and then its lacy leaves glow red. Those who believed in 'the doctrine of signatories' – that every plant by its appearance suggested its medicinal use – readily saw that this red plant should be used to stem bleeding. Above us is an ash tree. The wood, I explain, is supple and very tough, so it is the chief wood used to make tool handles. It is one of the best burning woods, and its seeds, like bunches of keys, were once pickled by country wives and served with meats. Ash was the 'tree of life' in Norse mythology, which binds together with its roots, trunk and branches, hell, earth and heaven. I mention that part of the beautiful Norse stone cross at Gosforth is carved in a fair imitation of the ash bark. About the foot of the ash tree are the shamrock-like leaves of wood sorrel, now finished flowering, but I have everyone chewing the leaves of this to make the point that it was, and still is, a useful addition to salads as it has a sharp vinegar taste, much loved by country children as a thirst quencher. In the hedge is a holly bush. Its reputation as a 'holy tree' has great antiquity. This has probably much to do with its evergreen quality. Branches of holly were often cut in the Lake District as a winter feed for sheep. It is an important 'larder' for wintering birds too.

We go on and I point out that every flower, every plant, had its uses. Even the humble lichen on walls and tree trunks provided the dyes for woollen yarn. We are out of tune now. The man who made those stone axes long before the birth of Christ would know which plants provided food, whether root or seed. Set a modern man in the wilderness without food and he would soon starve. Peat diggers in Denmark some years ago exhumed remarkably preserved human bodies which had been preserved by the peat for 2,000 years. Examination of their stomach contents by scientists revealed the seeds of clover, ryegrass, buttercup, goosefoots, lady's mantle, yarrow, black nightshade, camomile, smooth hawksbeard, barley, linseed, gold-of-pleasure, knotweed – and that Yorkshire fog grass. In fact what one might find in a bird-seed packet today. The whole might have been ground and boiled into a gruel. The rather grim mixture must have kept early man supplied with the valuable vegetable supplement to fish, flesh and fowl. Analysis of the residue in bronze vessels of this period also showed that Iron Age man drank an alcoholic beverage made from barley, cranberry, and bog myrtle. Cranberry and bog myrtle grow together in the swamps of the Lake District and I am tempted to make an experimental brew one day.

We forget that all our modern vegetables have been developed from the wild. Why do we not eat Good King Henry (*Chenopodium bonus-henricus*) any more? Where it grows wild now by some of our village greens and church yards, it indicates that the settlement is very old. The vegetable was popular and easy to grow, and the young shoots, then the succeeding leaves, then the flowering heads, and no doubt the seeds too, were all eaten. Culpeper states that the flavour was superior to spinach.

I engage my walking party on the lanes in tasting and smelling as well as feasting their eyes. I notice the father of one family seems bored and uncooperative, although his children are enjoying the new experience. He becomes something of a challenge to me and I make sure that he gets a sniff of all the crushed leaves I offer. There is no spark of interest. Towards the end of the walk we smell my last example, a laurel leaf. I ask him and everyone what the smell reminded them of. The children suggested marzipan, someone else suggests nuts, a lady oil of almonds. The man shakes his head. It is some time afterwards when we have looked at more trees and flowers, and have crossed the road to Brockhole car park, when the man turns to me. There is a gleam in his eyes. He looks at me and snapped 'Custard!' At first I do not know what he is talking about and almost say, 'And rhubarb to you!'. Then I remember the laurel.

'Yes. That's it. Custard!' he says. 'Thank you!' and he walks away happy.

Bar Volunteers

There is no 'typical' mountain search. Every one is different. A team can rehearse procedure until the cows come
home, and put in hours of practical exercise, but at the
call-out we must rely on common sense and spontaneity. In
the case of a search when large resources of manpower are
called upon, it is often necessary to enlist any handy person
to help in the line-up, and the search headquarters might be
a parish hall, a schoolroom, a room at a pub, or a Methodist
chapel. And one has to be prepared for the unexpected...

I was late home that evening; it had been fine but was
beginning to drizzle. There was a message that there was a
call-out, and I should report to the Langdale valley where
search headquarters had been established at an hotel. I ate
something quickly and drove to Langdale. The searchers –
two teams – had been out for some time, and I thought that
as I was a little tired, and the weather was not exactly
promising, I might land myself with a nice cushy job in
search headquarters, handling the radios, or drawing up
search areas. There was no sign of any searchers in fact, and
I reported to Sid, who was in charge of the search. He told
me the story. A coach party had stopped at the hotel, the

driver had told his passengers that they could have tea and report back in thirty minutes. This they did, except for one man. He had not been with anyone and nobody knew him, but he was last seen heading up toward the crags in the direction of the Pikes. The bus driver had waited an hour. The landlord told him that he had better go as the coach was keeping other customers out. The driver explained and they waited another half hour. That was enough, there were signs of restiveness amongst the other passengers and he moved off. The landlord felt it his duty to call out the rescue team, just in case this character had done something foolish. A quick check of the crags was fruitless so then Sid had called out the Kendal team to support the Langdale team.

'Personally,' said Sid, 'I don't think the man's up there. He's skived off. But we can't take chances. He may have fallen and be lying up there badly injured.'

'Pity everyone's out,' I said. 'I can hardly go on my own. I'll make myself useful here.'

'Don't worry about that,' said Sid. 'I'll find you a team. Come on into the bar.'

We walked into the bar and there was a number of drinking people dressed as if they had been fell walking. Sid could be persuasive. When he explained the situation and asked for volunteers to help in a search, eight people said they were willing. We ruled two of them out because they had no boots.

'Well John,' said Sid, 'there's six. Brief them, call at the ops room and I'll give you a radio.'

I looked at them. There was one man in his seventies. He was fit and well equipped and had been walking for years. But he admitted to being tired as he had done Scafell Pike that day. Then there was a young man called Eddy, in patched climbing breeches, his anorak covered in mud, and his face covered in hair. He said that he was fit as a fiddle. He was bouncing about as he talked and I believed him. He admitted to leading rock climbs to the 'very severe' standard. I told him that we would not be rock climbing but he would be a handy aid. There were also two students, one of whom was an Australian. They were novices; in fact they confessed that they had been lost themselves that day. Finally there was a young couple, quiet and well mannered, both fell club members with some experience. I told them that the job would be fairly easy. We would be given a search area and we would be keeping together in a line covering the ground. We still had some daylight left but we would have hand torches available.

We gathered round the map with Sid. He explained that he would like us to go up to the crags and sweep along the contours under them. The area had been searched before, but very quickly and not thoroughly, with only three men. Other searchers would be above us on the summits, more were working below. He gave us a radio, told us our call-sign, and we gathered bags of sandwiches and had flasks filled with tea. Then we took off upwards, slithering on the rock greased by the light rain. Our colleagues on the summits would be in mist. We were all right, but we had only about one hour of decent daylight left, and it would take us a half hour before we even reached our search area. Reach it we did, however, and we paused for a breather just under walls of crag. Joe, our oldest member, was puffed and said nothing. The young couple were also very quiet. Eddy was in animated conversation with the two students, telling them about what he had done and what he was about to do in the climbing world.

When we got our breath back I lined them up on contours. Joe took the lower line, below the young couple, Eddy the top one above the students, because if he was as nippy as he suggested, he was going to have to explore at least part way up the gulleys between the rocks, then drop back to rejoin us. We had a radio message to say that one group of searchers, having completed one search area, would be directly below us on another line. Michael, leader of this group, reminded us very cheekily that he did not want any boulders kicking down onto them. I passed the message on. We moved off.

We kept the line pretty well but I had to remind them that they were searching so it was not just a matter of looking where they put their feet. Eddy was fairly running up the gullies chattering back to us all the time, and hopping about like a frantic chamois. Occasionally I had to slow everyone to allow him to return and keep in line. I was not too happy about Joe; he looked to be limping and probably had a blister developing. The male member of the young couple had occasionally to give a hand to his partner over large obstacles and that worried me a bit too. These fears and having to handle the radio and a heavy pair of night binoculars meant that I was not doing much searching. We continued in this fashion until the light began to fade and eventually, from my position in the middle of the line, I was not able to see my end men clearly. I could, however, hear Eddy shouting and chattering from the crag base, dutifully telling us when he was leaving for an exploration and asking us to hold fire. I got worried about Joe eventually and, asking the students to relay any calls from Eddy down to me, I descended past the young couple. As I feared, Joe was missing and the couple said that they had not seen him for some time. Probably gone lame, I said, and could not keep up. I radioed down to Michael in the group below, told him I had a man missing, gave them his description, and asked them to keep a look out. I received a sardonic laugh and a rude comment back.

The light was now running out. It was just possible to make out a great wall of rock above us and I assumed, correctly I was relieved to find later, that it was Gimmer. Then came the message, 'No use endangering your men. Abandon search until morning. Come directly down to Mickleden.' I had just decided that we would have to turn back to look for Joe, when the message came from Michael.

'We've found your man. We've slapped a plaster on his heel and he's coming down with us.'

I breathed a long sigh of relief. But it was short lived. The students called down that they had lost contact with Eddy. I told them to stay put, and taking the young couple with me, we ascended to them. We lit torches and prepared to search. But first I called loudly and to our relief we heard Eddy reply; he seemed a long way off. Then I saw a light from a head torch way above us.

'Come on down, Eddy,' I called, 'we're abandoning search. Take care!'

The answer came 'Below!' and an assortment of boulders and stone grape-shot came in our direction. We took what shelter we could behind rock blocks and prayed. It went past.

'Sorry!' called Eddy gaily. 'Are you all right?'

'Frightened!' I shouted back. 'Take it steady!'

We remained in shelter and waited. Eventually he joined us.

'Sorry about the rocks!' he laughed.

I told everyone to get out their flasks and have a bite to eat. We were all looking pretty wet but we were warm with perspiration, and thirsty. I took out my vacuum flask.

'Put that away,' said Eddy, quietly to me. 'I've got something better than that.' He produced from a side pocket of his rucksack the remains of a half bottle of whisky. I then realised with horror that all this man's

250

chatter and capering about in dangerous gullies, and what I had taken for exuberant eccentricity, came from the man's inebriation. The thought made my hair stand on end. He could easily have been killed. He could have killed us. I felt it my duty to finish the bottle off there and then and I handed him my tea.

'This would be better for you now,' I said. 'And you'll stick close to me on the way down. O.K.?'

It was a painfully slow business descending over sometimes loose, always wet rock and very steep ground to the valley by the light of our torches. Each one of us at one stage or another fell and picked ourselves up. Eddy was now pretty hopeless and grabbed hold of my anorak from time to time. His chatter had become slurred. The students were still in good spirits but the couple slowed us down somewhat; they were now showing signs of fatigue. I was relieved when the message came through that the rescue Land Rover was coming to pick us up when we reached the valley floor. That would save us a mile's walk.

It seemed a long time before the ground under our feet levelled off. Eddy was now leaning on me and showing signs that he might drop off to sleep given half the chance. The girl was limping and being helped by her very tired partner. The Australian student admitted that his legs were beginning to feel like jelly and suggested that if he were a horse a humane vet would probably put him down. Then the glorious Land Rover arrived. Sid looked out of the driver's window and grinned.

'What's the matter John?' he said. 'You look tired!'

I retorted with something which I thought fitted the occasion.

More tea or hot soup in the ops room. Everyone looked a bit weary.

'I still don't think he's up there,' I said.

Sid said he was inclined to agree but the man's name and address had been traced and police checks at his home in a Lancashire town showed that he was still missing. Next thing was to wait for daylight. Sid called the teams to be on standby for 6.00 a.m.

'I trust you will be with us,' he said to me. 'I'll offer you a bed if you like.' I declined. It was 1.00 a.m.

'Best let this man sleep it off on some bench somewhere though,' I suggested, nodding to Eddy who was now sitting on the floor in a corner snoring noisily into his beard.

'Are you all right?' I asked the couple. The girl was slumped wearily with her head on her partner's shoulder.

'Yes,' replied the young man. 'We're staying here.' He grinned and added quietly to me. 'We were married this morning – sorry yesterday morning.'

'You shouldn't have come!' I gasped.

He smiled. 'It's a honeymoon night like no other!'

'How were your team?' asked Sid.

'First class,' I said, 'couldn't ask for a better.'

At 5.00 a.m. the bedside telephone rang to tell me the search was off as the man had turned up at his home having hitch-hiked. The next day, interviewed by a national daily and asked for his comments on the trouble he had caused, he was reported to have said that he decided on impulse to go for a walk and when he had seen the coach drive away as he was on his way back he decided to walk on and try to get a lift home. He finally made it about two in the morning and he criticised the rescue teams for turning out at all and making such a fuss. He said that he could look after himself. He had served in the marines. There was no suggestion of gratitude.

I was somewhat comforted to hear later that the local policeman watching the man's home on that night, and knowing the trouble that he was causing, did not approach the man when he saw him arriving at his door. He let him get inside. He watched the bedroom light go on and then off. He left the scene and attended to other duties for an hour or so – then went back and hammered on the man's door and got him out of bed. It was some consolation.

White Moss Tarn

Any place connected with William Wordsworth, however tenuously, has to be revered. Someone wrote to complain about the state of White Moss Tarn. The Wordsworths, it was said, had skated on it; nowadays it was so covered with weed there was no water to be seen. I was asked to get a volunteer work party together and do something about it. At the same time a research biologist was asked to make a report on why the tarn had weeded up so much. I made my own investigation too. I asked an old local inhabitant if the Wordsworths really had skated there.

'White Moss Tarn?' he scoffed as he paused from scything thistles. 'That's nowt but a mucky puddle! If anyone skated on that they'd spend half their time hitting t' banks.'

Well, it was a little tarn, and it was contained by a man-made bank and a little dam. It probably at one time provided a controllable stream of water for a mill below. It was completely choked by *Equisetum*, the horsetail. Horsetail is a weird plant in an order of its own, with long tubular jointed stems which come apart when pulled. It has no leaves, just whorls of tendril-like stems. The stem is shiny

254

as it is completely coated with a sheath of silica. Country wives used to use bunches of horsetail to scour and clean pots and pans. Of such kind of plants, the *Sphenopsids*, were our coal measures made, but then the plants grew as high as forty metres, and that was over 245 million years ago. The plant, remaining little changed in form if not in bulk, has worked out a marvellous system for survival. In fossil form it made a huge contribution to the start of the industrial revolution. Some experimental tugs at the crop in the pond convinced me that the volunteer labour was going to work up a fair head of steam too.

Put it about that there is a mucky job to do, like wading thigh deep in mud and water and cutting weed, and there is strangely no shortage of volunteers. It makes a change from pushing a pen or bending over a workbench. I got the loan of a dozen sets of rubber waders from the laboratories of the Freshwater Biological Association, and with two large wheelbarrows, rakes, forks and a dozen sickles, and with a great deal of optimism, we all assembled at the tarn one fine summer morning.

The first thing to do was to open up the dam sluice and lower the water to a workable depth. Soon, looking like clowns in oversize trousers, we stood around waiting for the first man to venture in. Mike was first. We watched with fascination as he walked in and then slowly sank in the oozy bottom mud until the water was above his knees and the horsetail above his waist.

'I've touched bottom,' he assured us. 'No problem except that I doubt if I can move.'

Soon we were all in and quickly discovered that the sickles were useless. It was doubtless more effective to get down to pulling the stuff out by the roots. This was not easy though. If you pulled from above water the stems merely pulled out of their sheaths. What you had to do was to throw off your shirt and get your arms well below water so that the hands could grasp the plants as near their roots as possible. The roots, great tangled rhizomes, broke of course, but a lot of them came away with a satisfying squelch. However, the activity stirred up the mud and there was a rich smell of decaying vegetable matter. It was a fine warm day and the sweat on the men (and the perspiration on the ladies) together with this rich cosy smell attracted squadrons of flies. Attempts to brush them off face and head produced streaks of mud which caused some cursing and some merriment, and produced more flies.

We worked well and cheerfully on the whole, and gradually began to reach the deeper centre of the tarn. Then I found myself watching Tom's face which was slowly changing to a grimace of horror. We saw at once what had happened. He had got in too deep, he was stuck, and the water had reached the top of his waders and was beginning to pour slowly but inexorably down his trouser legs. There was nothing he could do except utter a strangled cry as his neighbours shrieked with laughter. Soon several pairs of hands were pulling at him until he managed to extricate himself and stagger slowly, squelchily and awkwardly to the bank. Work stopped as we all watched him waggle onto the high ground. When he sat down to take off the waders the water gushed out causing horror on his part and hysteria on ours.

We all were to suffer Tom's fate. The only consolation was that the muddy water was fairly warm, and the sun was quickly drying. We found that the plants, once uprooted, floated on the surface and could be raked to the bank and forked out into the wheelbarrows. The biggest job was wheeling the stuff away to a dumping ground in a nearby swamp.

After several hours those of us who had not brought

rubber gloves were suffering from sore hands. We were aware too of an all-pervading smell, *Equisetum* or Horsetail – long considered a beneficial herb. Put in the bath-water, it is supposed to rapidly heal sores, wounds and shingles, and to soothe pain. Its vapours are said to clear the nose and chest. Taken inwardly it is considered to be a cure for diarrhoea and internal bleeding. I reckoned that one day of working amongst it would keep us fit for a long time. But there were several more days to come before we got it beaten and finally saw a sheet of rather greasy-looking water, and were able to close the sluice.

The researcher at the end of his learned treatise concluded that the increase in weed growth since Wordsworth's day was due to an enrichment of the water from nearby septic tank effluents. I told this to the old local inhabitant. He looked at me as if he did not know what a septic tank was and shook his head.

'Ducks,' he said.

'Ducks?'

'It were t' duck pond, wasn't it? They used to eat all t' weed. Then the new duck pond was made down below, opposite farm gate. They liked that better, so off they took to it and left White Moss Tarn. That's why t' weed grew.'

Ullswater Sunday

There is a haze in the still of early morning and the distinct feeling that it is going to be a hot day. Sunday too, and that means that as well as the holidaymakers there will be a large influx of day visitors. It is with some mixed feelings that I drive over to Ullswater for a lake patrol for the pressures on the lake are going to be tremendous and a warden will have to be somewhere in the middle doing his bit to sort out the chaos. It is a police duty. It is a job I would rather leave to a colleague. After all, I tell myself, you need a man who knows a lot about boats, and boating. But when duty calls we must not flinch. (Apart from that there is no one else available to do it.)

Kirkstone Pass is quiet, hardly any traffic at all, but I know it is the stillness before the storm. Ullswater flat calm and there is already the distant drone of a motor boat. The first of those who seek their recreation from the lake, are already there in some numbers. The anglers are always first and inevitably as the day goes on and other lake users spoil their sport, many will give up in disgust. But this is their hour.

John, the voluntary warden who is to be my partner on

the boat, is waiting at the boathouse at the northern end of the lake with his bait-bag and waterproofs. The place is unlocked, the cover taken from the boat, and I fill the fuel tank. Ventilate the engine-compartment for a few moments, then press the starter and she roars into life. Put on life-jackets, and we ease out into the lake. A call on the radio to say we are on duty and leisurely run up the long lake to Glenridding first. It seems a pity to violate the placid water; even at this speed the screw has boiled up the water astern and a wake is spreading out to jog the anglers' floats. An appreciative view of Place Fell on the left, its steep slopes covered in trees – one day I must explore. Glencoynedale above, a huge hollow in the hillside on the starboard bow, the classic glaciated valley, then as we turn at Silver Point the foothills of Helvellyn and Fairfield. Tie up at Glenridding Pier by the passenger 'steamer', now alas diesel. A chat with the skipper.

'Aye, it's goin' to be a fair day. 'Bout time too. It's only been a middlin' season so far. Glad to see you've got the reef markers out. They'll need another lick o' paint soon though. No we've had no trouble at Howtown pier lately. The ski-club have our timetable, I suppose, and there's only the odd cowboy.'

Ashore first to fill the fuel cans and collect lake by-law leaflets, and speak to the men who are emptying the litter baskets and cleaning yesterday's mess. Traffic is now building up, cars are streaming into the car park. There is a queue of cars on the road, and a few are pulling boat-trailers, some with boats and canoes and inflatables on the roof-racks. John looks at me and grins. These are only coming from the south. Many more will be coming down to the lake from the Penrith junction on the motorway.

There is a ripple on the lake when we get back. A slight wind getting up from the north-west, which should please the yacht club. Passengers are embarking on the steamer. Rowing boats and hired motor boats are beginning to venture out into the bay.

'Well,' remarks John, 'everyone's smiling.'

Untie, push off, restart and head slowly towards the islands. John points, but I've already seen him. Distant white moving spray with the nose of a fast boat in view heading for us. Well, this is the first. I open the throttle and move to intercept. Our distance rapidly narrows. Before we meet I turn in front of him. He cannot avoid seeing me and seeing our large 'Warden' sign on the side. He slows down. I turn to fall in with his speed and move alongside.

'Are you new to the lake?'

'First time, yes.'

'Remember this then. You're in a ten miles an hour restricted zone. Have a look at this leaflet which shows the speed limit areas. You see up at this end of the lake there are a lot of slow hired craft and rowing boats. The by-laws have been made in the interests of safety.'

'Right. O.K. Thanks.'

A slow look around, while John records the incident. Nothing much happens for a while. One or two small inflatables on the shore. We move in and warn some parents not to let their children float too far away. Another group is also warned that it is unwise to allow their children to paddle about the shore with bare feet – there are sharp stones and possibly some litter-louts' broken glass. All our advice followed with 'Have a good day.' The sun is now getting pleasantly warm, and everyone still smiling.

Another lull and then the peace shattered by a roar behind us from the area back at the pier. A large fast yellow boat has been launched and is heading our way at around thirty miles per hour. Open up again to intercept, turn broadside to his course and he throttles down. Fall in alongside.

'Have you been on this lake before?'

'No.'

'Did you not see the lake by-law sign on the shore?'

'No.'

'Do you always launch onto a lake without first getting information about safety regulations?'

He shrugs. We give him a leaflet and make another entry in the log.

We head out of the speed limit area and we are at once into greater activity. There is noise, a lot of moving spray. Spray from the fast boats, spray from water-skiers behind them. Six boats operating from the west shore. They could not have launched from there but have deposited people and gear on an area normally used by picnic parties only. Those who do not like noise and motor boats will move on if they have not already. There is nothing much we can do about it. There is no by-law against boats operating from the shallows – only against launching. Two anglers are grimly sitting it out on a small crag. It will not be long before they give up.

John points into the water ahead. There is an area of bubbles. A skin-diver emerges, then another. I wave and move in closer. I give the diver a warning about operating too near fast motor boats and point out that they have no marker buoy and the boat owners may have no idea where they are diving.

'We were here first,' grumbles the man in a smart red outfit.

'I'm sorry. We can't do much about that. I'm only thinking of your safety.'

John points out some small inflatables behind us. We move out to them. No life-jackets at all among the cheerful occupants. We warn them that the lake is 150 feet deep here

261

and that the water is very cold, and their craft very vulnerable. One of the craft is particularly worrying.

'That must have come out of a cornflakes packet,' John remarks to me.

As the motorboats come in we speak to the occupants and warn them to look out for other people and to try not to spoil their enjoyment. Even as we speak a boat roars in behind us and a water-skier lets his tow drop and zooms into land, showering a family of picnickers who have just arrived. He is not inclined to apologise. 'We were here before them.' I tell him that he and his boat crew could be prosecuted for inconsiderate navigation. Who was first is immaterial. It does not give them superior rights. Further, they must keep the boat in the water and not land it on the beach. If they do, they will be in breach of the National Trust by-laws. They say they understand and I suggest that if everyone considered other people's enjoyment there would be no trouble. 'Let's all have a good day.' I go astern and pull away, but I fear that the picnic party will eventually find the conflict unequal and move off.

Another craft zooms in towing a skier and I try to overcome my gloom as I intercept. There is only one man in the boat. I move in. I ask him how long they have been skiing.

'A year or so.'

'Then you must surely know that there is the basic safety rule that there should be two in the boat, one responsible adult to watch the skier, another to navigate.'

No, they do not know about the rule. I ask them if they see the sense of it. They agree. I point out that on this lake the rule has the force of law and if I see them without two in the boat again I will have to consider a prosecution. John gives them a leaflet. We leave them looking slightly gloomy.

The breeze has now increased, but it is still pleasantly

warm. We head into mid-lake at a moderate speed, and I speculate on how the ecology of the lake is affected by the human activity. Somewhere below in this deep water are shoals of schelly, a white fish, a sort of fresh-water herring which is peculiar only to this lake and Helvellyn's tarn. It is a relic of the Ice Age. Once, the main activity on the lake, apart from its use as a highway, was the netting of the schelly, for the fish is very good eating.

There is no trouble normally in mid-lake. Speed is de-restricted and the main yachting activity is at the foot of the lake. We approach Howtown Bay where the ski-club operates, pick up a drifting ski and carry it in. A boat comes to us and the grateful owner of the ski waves. No trouble here. The club knows the rules. Down to Sharrow Bay with some small apprehension, for we are entering the pressure region. Beyond is the yacht club shore which is within a speed limit area inside a boundary which crosses the lake obliquely. There are markers at both ends but so far apart that they cannot both be seen. A line of marker buoys is impractical owing to the water's depth. The line is an arbitrary one, a compromise no doubt, but practically impossible to enforce. John immediately points out a speeding boat coming through a yacht race and I open to intercept. We have hardly given him a leaflet and ascertained that he has come from the camp site beyond the yacht club, when another one tears across, and another. From now on it is intercepting and warning and logging for an hour. We move along the shore line of the camp site and I switch on the loud hailer.

'For the information of motor boat owners who may not have been on this lake before, you are in a speed limit area of ten miles per hour. You shouldn't go beyond that speed until you reach middle reaches of the lake. There are explanatory notices on the shore and there are leaflets

263

available from us or any information centre. The rules have been made in the interests of safety for all lake users. – Take care. – Have a good day.'

We are back to the yacht club area, watching the race, and for the first time notice how the wind has got up. Some of the boats are moving briskly and keeling in the gusts. We go round and into Sharrow Bay. I cut the engine and we drift inshore for lunch.

Sandwiches and coffee while John talks about boat-building. He built a boat indoors and eventually had to take out house windows and frame to get it out. It was clinker built and he was very relieved when he actually saw it floating and not leaking. He tries to explain how he built in buoyancy and stability. We reminisce then about queer incidents we have seen on the lake patrols. Fires on motor boats are common, and John describes how he saw one boat explode, throwing its occupants into the water 'like rag dolls', luckily with only minor injuries. The drill we have worked out is to concentrate on getting the boat occupants out of danger and to worry about the fire after that. We talk about capsizes. Normally capsizes of yachts are dealt with by their crew. Occasionally if the crew is not competent we have to move in and rescue, as the water is very cold, and people can soon be overcome. I tell him of one of my own classic incidents. It was Easter when the water was deadly cold and it was windy. I was watching one boat in particular handled by a man in wet-suit and life-jacket, but there was a passenger, an elderly man, I supposed his father, who was incongruously dressed in a tweed suit and a cloth cap; he had no life-jacket. The boat capsized in mid-lake and I moved in to pick up the elderly man. He was swimming and all right and was in fact trying to help his son haul the boat upright. I looked at my watch. I could only give him five minutes in this temperature, and then he would have to be hauled aboard. They got the boat upright but could not get in until they had baled out. At five minutes I called to the elderly man. 'Do you want any help?'

He looked at me with no sign of distress and answered in a hoarse but rich fruity Yorkshire voice. 'Aye – y'can. Can you find mi cap?'

After lunch we move into the lower reaches again. The behaviour has definitely improved now everyone knows we are about. Even so we find ourselves telling ski-towers that they must have two in the boat and a driving mirror, and we still have continuing speeding offences. To two we give final warnings, for it is their second violation. The sun is now quite warm and we have to have friendly warning words with drifting sunbathers being blown out on inflatables and parents not watching their children. The behaviour improves still more, so we move up-lake to see what is happening there.

Everything is happening. John picks up binoculars then points to a dark shape on the starboard bow. As we speed nearer we see that it is a blue canoe with its life-jacketed owner clinging to it. He waves to us, and we move alongside. I cut the engine.

'Can't right it.'

'Niver worry,' says John. 'You did right to stay with it. Climb aboard.'

We haul him aboard, bring the canoe closer and right it. John produces a line and ties the canoe to a lug. The lad is cold and demoralised so I give him a cup of coffee from my spare flask. It has a miraculous effect and we start the engine and move about looking for his missing paddle. It is surprising how far it has drifted away. We land him at Gowbarrow where his adventure started.

Then there are more speeding offences to deal with. On one I have to open up the throttle wide and we chase him at about forty miles an hour. The boat is planing – almost aeroplaning – and throwing us about like ping-pong balls. I do not like it all, but eventually we get alongside and I stop him with a call from the loud hailer. One of the speeding boats is piloted by a boy of ten years old. In this case we take the father's name and address and a report will be made with a view to prosecution. The boy is so small that it is impossible for him to see over the bows and verbal steering instructions were being given by his dad, well forward of him and certainly out of reach of controls.

We stop one man launching a power boat from land where it is prohibited by National Trust by-laws. I point out the offence and he puts it to me that if he launches his boat without the outboard engine fixed he would be within the law. Once he got off the land covered by the by-law he could then put on his engine. I tell him that is interesting and if he would like me to take it to court as a test case I would be more than willing to take his name and address, and pursue the matter. He says nothing more but begins to haul the boat up to his boat trailer.

For a change one sailing boat owner asks where he can get his boat ashore. I ask him where he launched; he points up a steep bank. He was helped, he said, by ten strong men from a coach which happened to be stopped at that point. He now reckons he needs twenty men to get him out. I tell him to go to a point up lake where the beach is almost at road level.

We speak to the gay occupants of a very overloaded boat. It appears they have also taken on a load of beer. We steer them inshore and hope for the best. A family wave to us from a picnic beach.

'Our boy has drifted out. Can you bring him back?'

John searches with binoculars and points. I head out to round the lad up, and John hauls him and his flimsy

266

inflatable aboard. We speak to two power boat owners who are speeding too close to rowing boats. There are more speeding offences and the log book is getting full. We take the boy to shore.

We make the sweep down-lake past the yacht club and move past the camp site. The boat owners have got the message apparently and we move back to our boathouse and close down the radio. It is 17.30 and we decide to call it a day. We tie up, sponge the boat down and pick up empty fuel cans; then we secure the boat and leave it.

The roads now are busy with the home-bound day-trippers, contented after a fine day. We part and I pull in at Glenridding, finish my spare flask and wait awhile for the traffic to thin out. Over the Land Rover radio I listen to the conversation of members of the Patterdale Mountain Rescue team on a rescue. A man has fallen off Striding Edge. It has been a busy day on the fells too.

Farm Visit

The classic Lake District scene is there, all the living elements of it. Mountains crowded together, pushing and shoving into the skyline. Unstable crags, harassed by winter ice and frosts, spilling scree, shouldering aside falling becks which retaliate by scouring out deep scars. Trees and shrubs fighting for life, away from browsing animals, in the thin-soiled gullies. Green ground-cover of grasses, heather, ling and mosses struggling against the wearing action of heavy rainfall, frosts, winds, and exposure to dry summer sun. Below, the immaculate meadows, made, fertilised, limed, de-stoned for many years, fenced in by walls which stride for miles over the landscape. Below that, fingers of broadleaved woods, groups of trees and hedges, and there in the hollow the small farm house, sitting butt to wind in its clump of yew trees. Then all the lines of interest, slopes, crags, becks, walls, woods, all converging to the one great feature; the level lake. The great conciliator of all the opposing elements. The quivering light in the centre of the converging shades. It is a balance. There is not a single discord.

And yet man has had a hand in this landscape. Without

benefit of landscape architect or planners he has so far managed to avoid making straight-lined conifer plantations, and ruling out straight swathes of tarmac, or cluttering up exposed hillsides with buildings. He had made over a century or two or three a tolerably good job of adaptation. He is in tune.

I follow the fresh tractor tracks up through the lower fields of the inby, and through the open gates to the upper intakes. Some steers raise their heads from grazing and stare at me curiously, some fall into step behind me. The tractor tracks curve with the contours and there is the tractor at the far stone wall, with Bill working on a wall repair. He hardly looks up as I approach, a brief glance and a nod, and as I get closer a 'Hoo ista?' without stopping work.

'Not so bad. How are you?'

'Middlin' fair.'

I start collecting some of the collapsed wall stones which have rolled down the hill and drop them at the wall gap. We talk about the weather and his lambing season and eventually, after a decent time, I get to the point.

'You know why I've come to see you?'

He stops and grins and says 'No', but I think he knows well enough.

'Somebody's complained about your bull again; on that bottom field with the public footpath through it.'

'That bull wouldn't hurt a fly.'

'We know that. I've just walked by it. But other folk don't know. It's agin the law in this country to have a bull in a field with a right of way through it.'

'Hear tell they're gooin' to change t' law.'

'They haven't yet.'

'Tell you what. Most visitors can't tell a bull if they see yan. Reckon it's sartin locals complainin' agin?'

269

'There's been a complaint. I have to follow it up.'

'It's a hardship. I've got to run a bull with those coos.'

'Aye, I know. It has to be behind fences.'

He has not stopped working and he continues thoughtfully clonking on the stones. I have to ask him eventually if he is going to move the bull. He turns and grins. I think he is enjoying my discomfort.

'Reckon so. Finished with that field anyway.'

I lug up some cam stones and he begins to cap the wall, tightens the barbed wire on the top and the repair is complete. He leans on it, takes off his cap to scratch his head and we both look down and across the valley to the lake.

'I reckon you have the best view of any farm in these parts,' I say.

'Reckon so.' He smiles. 'Wife reckoned she married me 'cos I raved aboot t' view, and very near left me when I browt her and she foond she couldn't see it from t' hoose!'

'How many generations of your family have lived here?'

'Fower.'

'You were brought up here and yet you still appreciate the view?'

He looks puzzled for a moment, then says, 'Put it this way. Family's nivver made money off this land. But we've nivver starved either.' He loads wire and tools on his tractor and whistles his dogs. 'Where are you off till now?'

'Up the hill. Still have trouble with those sheep folds up there?'

'It's campers. They have to take off t' cam stones to howd down their tents from t' wind. Nivver put 'em back. Bloody nuisance.'

'I'll have a look.'

He nods, climbs onto the tractor, waves, and he is off down the hill with the dogs padding about. I look again at

270

the view. It is a coming together of all the thrusting, struggling elements. I look down the faultless green fields which are an essential part of all this. It is all a coming to terms. A cooperation. A sharing. But it is still a struggle, seven days a week. Hard back-breaking graft. A bit of cunning helps too.

Finale

The odd thing about beautiful landscape is that people are often afraid to look at it raw. They will be riveted by a natural history programme on television, and these are always rated highly in the surveys of viewing figures. Lectures on landscape and nature with well-produced colour slides at Brockhole, our National Park Visitor Centre, are invariably the most popular. They are shown to stimulate interest and an urge to go out and see. But I fear that many cannot see without help. It is almost as if the human eye cannot take in a scene unless it is in a frame. If I project my colour slides in an introductory talk at Brockhole there are sometimes suitable noises of appreciation. (I take so many photographs there are bound to be one or two that are fairly good.) On the walk the group can unknowingly walk past the view, the coloured shadows of which they had only a little while ago admired.

We need frames. There is nothing new in this, although nowadays one might be tempted to put the blame on our addiction to television. The early tourists to the Lake District were advised to carry a mirror in a pretty frame, and on reaching the recommended viewpoint they were required to stand with their backs to the view and hold the mirror up. Or they could use a 'Claude glass' (named after the seventeenth-century landscape artist?), a frame containing a sheet of coloured glass. They could buy a selection of framed glasses pinned together at a corner, and then it was possible to look at the classic view suitably isolated by the frame and highlighted in pale blue, green, yellow or pink glass – whichever they fancied.

A view from a window is easily appreciated, while outdoors, with it all wrapped around the viewer in three dimensions, it might be too much to take in. Approach Glencoe from the south on a clear day by the public road and one can hardly fail to be impressed by one of the most dramatic of Scotland's scenes. But see Buachaille Etive Mor from that magnificent lounge window in the nearby Kings House Hotel and you may well get goose-pimples with shocked excitement. It must take the prize for the most awe-inspiring window view of any place in Britain, and if you have first moistened your palate with a glass of old single-malt I swear that you might hear fanfares of silver trumpets! But perhaps that is very strong meat for many. Alas for the death of the old Anglers' Hotel, murdered in the cause of water supply, with its peaceful view from the dining-room window across Ennerdale Water lapping close beneath, to the skyline of Pillar, Scoatfell and Steeple, with little sign of human intrusion. The view is still there; the hospitable frame has gone.

We have for so long had our attention imprisoned within window frames and screens that when we come out blinking under the bright skylight of the vast outdoors we have to adjust, we have to learn to appreciate it all at once – the pure moving air, the land, water and skyscape, the scent and the sounds. One needs to be still and let it come in slowly to the consciousness as the incoming tide seeps and

273

sings in to the dry sand. It is a technique we need to learn. And having learned we have to practise. For even those of us who are fortunate to see beautiful countryside every day are often blind to it. I once remarked to a friend of mine how wonderful the foam of blackthorn blossom was that year in the hedge against his home.

'I hadn't noticed,' he said. 'Maybe I'm getting old.'

As I left him I thought, 'Friend, you are not getting old. You are dead, dead, dead!'

Going out in the quiet morning I can turn a corner and behind the woods, across the green meadows beyond the big ash tree, there is the level lake, and away biting into the horizon the high terraces, towers and pinnacles of Langdale Pikes. They are always there but never the same. The colours change with the seasons, and they respond hourly to the light and the pattern of cloud shadows. And on this summer morning with a light breeze, and a blue sky and a blackbird practising his piece I can remind myself of the passage in Isaiah, 'For ye shall go out with joy and be led forth with peace, the mountains and the hills shall break forth before you into singing, and all the trees of the field shall clap their hands. Behold I make all things new.'

The passage is perfect, for I certainly go out with joy in the gentle warmth of the sun, and it is the peace and quietness that lead me forth (as well as the necessity of the day's work), and the mountains and the hills do break forth before me as I turn the corner, and they surely sing. Wherever there is harmony, order and proportion it sings and there is joy in the experience of it. And the trees certainly clap their hands as their leaves are lightly stroked by the warm wind; the birches gaily, the oaks sedately, the thorns solemnly, the aspen madly. What a clapping and a singing!

If the music is not always gay it is always beautiful.

274

Wordsworth, on contemplating 'an evening of extraordinary splendour and beauty in the vale of Grasmere' saw in it a 'deep and solemn harmony'. The sunsets are surely the most beautiful for, like Wordsworth's from Dove Cottage, my views to the west have the hills and mountains in them, and there is a strange pull in that west, a feeling of regret that the mountains are swallowing up another day. A desire to climb and follow it. And in the sunset hour even the trees clapping their hands have a sadness in them. If the wind is strong from the west there is a wild abandoned throwing of arms and shaking of heads, but it is a farewell to the day still, an Irish wake. Sometimes if the song is a hushed humming there is a sad swaying, a moving of fingers, a gentle touching.

These are, I suppose, according to the mood of the weather and the watcher, Beethovian experiences of landscape, or Vivaldian, Holstian, or Wagnerian. There can be extreme operatic drama. I was once leading a party of Londoners from Helvellyn over Dollywaggon in mist and rain and strong wind. The struggle with the elements had been a great disappointment to them. They had had dull misty weather for the several days of their stay. They had looked forward for weeks to the fell walk, and after leaving the cars in Patterdale they had seen nothing. Helvellyn, but for the exertion of the climb and the last scramble to the ridge, might have been Box Hill. Then as we approached Dollywaggon's southerly descent the rain ceased and the mist in front of us glowed a pale yellow. I knew what was coming, the others did not. I heard the song, first the soft whisper of it, the muted harmonies, then the drum-beats, growing, growing – swelling. Then with a great crash the mighty orchestra burst forth to a crescendo at the dramatic sweep of the Almighty's baton – the curtain of mist was plucked savagely back and tore above our heads as the great trumpet-roar of the wind struck us. Suddenly out of obscurity there was the almost painfully vivid view of the flank of Fairfield, golden with sunshine and animated with racing cloud shadows, and dizzily far below at our feet, the grey-blue waters of Grisedale Tarn, whipped with white furrows. The great anthem roared out to us – 'Glory! Alleluia!' A shout of surprise came from my party and it was not just the wind that made them sit down; the experience left them powerless to move. One of us lost a hat. I swear it was thrown in the air! I looked around at the faces. There was astonishment, elation, shock. It was an unforgettable moment.

Sometimes in committee rooms of the National Park Authority, and of the National Trust, in which I am privileged to serve, I join with good well-intentioned people to talk about countryside conservation. I am grateful for the efforts of those who serve with me professionally and voluntarily. But when I listen to them I have sometimes a tinge of apprehension. For I fear that the countryside is being discussed as an abstract. It has to be evaluated, labelled, filed; and there are problems and options and management plans. Sometimes it seems that the land owners, the farmers, the politicians, the conservationists and the recreationalists sound like an estranged family arguing over the custody of a child. It is just my fancy, of course, for I am not a happy committee man, though I am sure that committees are necessary in the interests of fairness. And although I can say my piece dutifully, sometimes I am really back in my schoolroom and back to my old frustrations at being kept in, for outside the committee room window I can see a poplar tree clapping its hands in time to the distant song.

But landscape is not to be preserved only for its own sake. It is there to lead people forth in peace. 'People need the refreshment which is obtainable from the beauty ... of unspoiled country.' Actually Father Thomas West, a local priest who wrote one of the first guide books to the Lake District in 1778, expressed it well: 'Such as spend their lives in cities, and their time in crowds, will here meet with objects that will enlarge the mind by contemplation and raise it from nature to nature's first cause. Whoever takes a walk into these scenes must return penetrated with a sense of the Creator's power in heaping mountains upon mountains, and enthroning rocks upon rocks. And such exhibitions of sublime and beautiful objects, cannot but excite at once both rapture and reverence.'

Well, Father, you may be right. When I observe the holiday pressures on the National Park, I see an abundance of rapture. But I feel that the future lies in cultivating a good deal more reverence.